Wildflowers in the Median

Emma,

Wildflowers in the Median

❦

A Restorative Journey into
Healing, Justice, and Joy

AGNES FUREY AND LEONARD SCOVENS

Best wishes,
Agnes Furey

iUniverse, Inc.
Bloomington

Wildflowers in the Median
A Restorative Journey into Healing, Justice, and Joy

iUniverse books may be ordered through booksellers or by contacting:

iUniverse
1663 Liberty Drive
Bloomington, IN 47403
www.iuniverse.com
1-800-Authors (1-800-288-4677)

ISBN: 978-1-4759-5367-1 (sc)
ISBN: 978-1-4759-5368-8 (hc)
ISBN: 978-1-4759-5369-5 (e)

Printed in the United States of America

iUniverse rev. date: 11/05/2012

For Pat, Chris, and Andre

"There is no linear path with an end on which to travel. Rather, the healing path is a winding one; some may pass the same spot more than once."

—Barb Toews

Contents

Foreword

A journey of restoration begins with one person reaching out to another. In this case, the person is Agnes Furey reaching out to Leonard Scovens, the man who murdered her child and her grandchild. How did she find it in her heart to open herself to writing Leonard? How did she choose peace rather than hate?

I met Agnes twelve years ago when she attended my writing class at Tallahassee Memorial Hospital Women's Center. The unthinkable had just happened, and she was reeling from the aftershocks of the laceration to her psyche. She had come to write. She had come to heal. In the years since, Agnes has continued to attend my classes and has revealed herself to be not only a powerful writer but an agent of transformation for others. She speaks her own truth with a vigilant beauty that has inspired many.

I've met Leonard only through the words in this book, which—as you shall see—paint a portrait of a complex, sensitive, articulate, and humble human being who has sought to overcome his violent history. This is Agnes's and Leonard's story in poems, vignettes, and letters. It is a tale not of forgiveness but of understanding, a story of a so-called victim and a so-called perpetrator finding common ground as they struggle with their own grief and suffering and as they begin to come to terms with their own spiritual identities and shared desire to help others in similar circumstances.

To read their words is to step into an arena seldom visited, to engage with souls that hold nothing back, and to open oneself to the wisdom of the pen and the hand that holds it. This is an unlikely and valuable testament to the human heart and its capacity to love. I invite you to engage fully with what Agnes and Leonard have to teach us. In their restorative journey lies hope for us all.

Katya Sabaroff Taylor is a writer and writing teacher who has volunteered in prisons. She is the author of the forthcoming book Prison Wisdom, *an anthology of writings from inmates.*

Introduction

To understand something about how one person can forgive and how another can kill, we must know something essential about ourselves. What makes the forgiver different from most of the rest of us, who want to kill the killer in the name of justice? What makes the killer different from most of the rest of us, who only sanction killing as an act of either revenge or protection? Or are they really different from any of us at all? Don't we all begin by loving our mothers, worshipping our fathers, tolerating our siblings, and crawling before we walk? When do we diverge? Where in our journey can we find the moment that determines whether we will kill or forgive?

Let Me Introduce Myself

I am me.
I am a woman who has lived long.
I am a survivor of homicide and suicide.
I am a grandparent and great-grandparent.
I am a poet and a writer.
I am.

January 2007

When I Was Nine

You, Momma, held me down beneath the weight of your behind
while he slashed his extension cord into my back, thighs, arms.
I struggled under you and couldn't breathe. The blood
running down the valleys and grooves carved into my skin
smelled like one hundred wet pennies. I slipped from under you, ran
and jumped down two flights of stairs, thinking, *I gotta get away*
gotta run gotta get the hell outta here
can't let them hit me no more.

Your feet slapped the hardwood floor
in counterpoint to his work boots pounding down the stairs behind me
pushing me fasterfasterharderfaster as I ran.

You were so close but I had to make it. *Gotta get away*
gotta run gotta get the hell outta here.
I saw the blue-jean sky and blond sun so clear and clean through the window,
so pretty and sweet and nice and everything apple pie American,
and I had to make it so I jumped.

And the goddamned glass didn't break.
Like my bones wouldn't shatter no matter how hard you hit me;
no matter how many times he slammed that two-by-two into my head
it wouldn't crack, my brains wouldn't spill free.

> *somebody make it stop please make it*
stop
He made me shower afterward to rinse the wounds

and I shivered beneath the cold water praying he wouldn't hit me no more,
                              Andre crying behind me.
so sorry i got you into this shit, little brother, so sorry, so sorry i'm so bad;
i'm so badbadbad and so sorry i can't kill this crazymotherfucker with the
two-by-two.

I saw white fire and little electric flowers when he slammed that slab of
wood into my head,
his voice booming behind it,
Get your punk ass under that water, little nigger!

This must be what it's like when you die—
                              the voice of God judging you,
punishing you for all the bad shit you've done.
If so, I don't want no parts.
I done seen enough hell to know it can't be no more fucked up than this.

Gathering the Pieces

I remember a room, a living room, in the two-room apartment where Pat and Chris had lived.

David, Pat's former husband, and I had the task of sorting through what was there, what was left of their lives. The bookcase and couch were out of place, the TV table barren, the TV/VCR gone.

A search warrant, newspapers, mail, notes, a church bulletin, and kindergarten drawings were strewn on the coffee table and floor with no pattern or meaning, just as the investigators had left them.

We tried sitting on the couch and couldn't. Standing, we silently fingered through the papers. We couldn't yet speak; we could barely look at each other. Finally, we sat on the floor. Tentatively, at first, one of us would make a comment and then the other. We talked as we sorted; we remembered; we shared old and new stories, feelings, sadness, horror, and disbelief; and we bonded, as only we could. We, each of us, loved them in our own way.

January 24, 2006

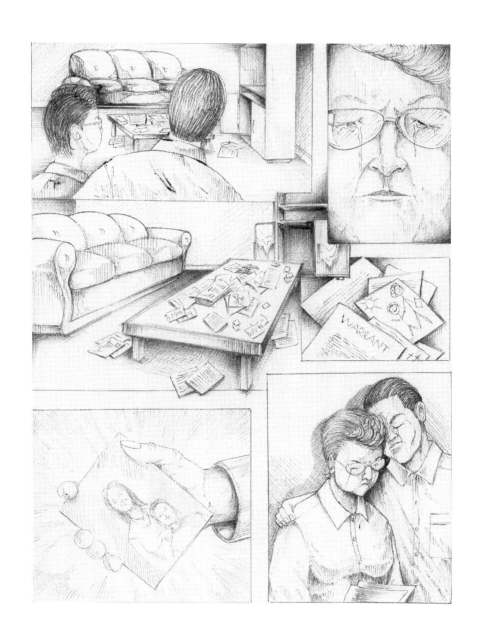

A Statement To The Court
On Behalf Of
Patricia Ann Reed
July 7, 1957–March 23, 1998
and
Christopher Thomas Reed
November 7, 1991–March 23, 1998

In The Case Of Leonard Scovens
March 1, 1999

My name is Agnes Furey. I am the mother of three children and the grandmother of four. My youngest child, Margaret, died in 1960. My son, Frank, died in 1996. My oldest child, Pat, and my youngest grandchild, Christopher, were murdered in March 1998 by Leonard Scovens.

This (*gesturing to a woman in the audience*) is Loretta Bukowski, who is also Christopher's grandmother. Our families have all spoken over the last few days, and I hope to be speaking for all of them: Pat's older children, Jason and Alicia (Christopher always called them "my Jason" and "my Alicia"); her former husband and best friend, David Reed; Christopher's father, Alex Walters; my son's wife, Laurie, and their son, Mark; my brother, Gene; all of Christopher's teachers and classmates; Pat's many friends; and many others who have been affected.

Pat grew up in Jersey City, New Jersey, in what would now be called an inner city. She was a happy child, good in school. She loved music, especially the Monkees and the Jackson Five. She sang in the glee club. She enjoyed swimming and the beach, as well as camping in the pine barrens of New Jersey and ice skating in Central Park.

She had a special bond with her grandmother. Her father left when she was six. She and her brother had at least the usual rivalries and arguments of many siblings. They grew closer over the years.

We took advantage of the proximity of New York City. We attended children's theater, Shakespeare in Central Park, the New York Mets, and of course the World's Fair.

I particularly remember a long bus trip, just she and I, and a tour of historic Philadelphia.

As an adolescent and a young person, Pat had two attributes that continued in varying intensity throughout her life: a profound caring for all God's creatures and a problem with alcohol. Dogs, cats, and birds in differing number and combinations were usually in her life; most were strays she simply could not abandon. She also loved plants and grew vegetables at different times. She surely would have had a horse if the opportunity had presented itself.

Friends and acquaintances were seldom denied when they showed up with a problem. I remember a woman with three or four children who was fleeing an abusive husband and stayed with her for several months.

Her primary lifelong goal, from which she never wavered, was to be a mother. As a teenager, she went to Arizona to help her uncle Gene with his two daughters while his wife had surgery. It was in Jersey City that she met, dated, fell in love with, and then married David Reed. They moved to Norfolk, Virginia, where he was stationed with the navy. They had two children, Jason and Alicia. Jason is now sixteen, and Alicia is fourteen. They were her delight. Pat's kids were what she talked about and worried over.

Throughout, her problem with alcohol would sometimes surface. The time of the war in the Persian Gulf was especially difficult. Pat met Alex, Christopher's father, during this time.

Christopher was born. David gave him his name and loved him as his own. Jason and Alicia loved their baby brother. In time, Pat's marriage ended, but the family endured. As always, her kids remained her primary focus.

Then Alex entered Christopher's life, and a series of many visits to Grandma Retta began.

Pat's drinking became more problematic. David was transferred to Texas, and Pat and Chris were to stay with me in Tallahassee until she could be on her own.

In a very short time, it became necessary for her to be hospitalized. With the intervention of her brother and me and the assistance of friends, she entered into treatment. Although angry and resistant at first, she soon became engaged in the process and embraced sobriety.

Christopher came to live with me while his mother recovered. He entered preschool and flourished. We developed a loving and interesting relationship. He invigorated as well as exhausted me. He accompanied me to board meetings of the AIDS service organizations, crack cocaine seminars, church, and the market. I went to PTA meetings, played basketball, and attended parenting classes. Christopher was beloved by a community of Grandma's friends. It was said he had a talent for making his presence known.

And we traveled. In the eighteen months he was with me, we must have driven from Tallahassee to Sarasota fifty or sixty times. We visited Mommy when she was in treatment and then in the halfway house, as well as later in her one-room apartment and then in a larger apartment.

She first went to work on the bus, then a bicycle, a moped, and finally a car.

Sometimes we stayed at Uncle Frank's and Aunt Laurie's. Frank was becoming ill. When he was at hospice we visited every weekend. Christopher and his cousin Mark built forts with blankets and had their safe space together. We took Frank to Mark's soccer games when he was able to go.

Christopher's teacher told me that he reported all of the weekends' events to the class on Mondays. They observed a quiet moment when Christopher's uncle Frank died.

At Christmas a year after Pat went to treatment, all three of her kids were with her for the holiday break and again the following summer. The older ones, Jason and Alicia, then returned to their dad and school in Texas, and Christopher was reunited permanently with Pat.

They did well—he in school, she sober and working while taking home study courses and planning to move into a larger apartment. Again, her kids were her primary focus.

Her prayer, as she underlined it in the Big Book of Alcoholics Anonymous, was as follows:

God, I offer myself to thee to build with me and to do with me what thou wilt. Relieve me of the bondage of self, that I may better do thy will. Take away my difficulties that victory over them may bear witness to those I would help, of thy power, thy love, and thy way of life. May I do thy will always.

Grandma Retta moved to Largo, and Christopher visited on many weekends, swimming in the pool and camping in the backyard. They became buddies. As was his habit, he reported these events at kindergarten on Mondays.

Retta bought him a tuxedo, and he participated in Alex's wedding in Virginia.

Then ... what happened?

I first met Leonard outside of Walmart. Ever vigilant about confidentiality, Pat was careful just to say, "This is Leonard." I recall having an uneasy feeling that day. I later came to understand that this was someone she had met in treatment.

I next met him some months later at Pat's apartment. He was there for several days as he had left treatment and had no place to go. I felt fearful for her well-being, and we had quite a discussion. She said, "You always said everyone deserves a chance."

"But we are not required to provide them all," I replied.

Several days later, he disappeared with her VCR, which was not yet fully paid for. She was angry and felt betrayed but remained sober. We were grateful that was all that happened. He apparently returned to Baltimore.

Occasionally, Pat would mention that she had heard from Leonard. She didn't appear to harbor any resentment. She had been impressed with his artistic interests. I remember some mention of the Ringling School.

In early March of last year, Pat told me that Leonard had just gotten kicked out of the Job Corps and needed someplace to stay. I repeated my earlier caution that he was his own responsibility.

Soon after Pat and I had that conversation, Loretta met Leonard when she'd brought Christopher back to Pat's after having kept him for the weekend. She described the same sense of unease I'd felt upon meeting Leonard.

I called Pat several times that week without success. Either the line was busy or the voice mail did not come on.

Finally, very early Friday, after many calls to Sarasota's police department and sheriff's office, her place of employment, and my daughter-in-law, Laurie, two officers from Tallahassee's police department came to my job and informed me that Pat and Christopher had been murdered.

Loretta saw it on the noon news on TV.

Pat and Christopher are both dead! She was forty; he was six.

Countless lives have been shattered—mine and Retta's, David's and Alex's, Jason's and Alicia's, Laurie's and Mark's, Uncle Gene's, as well as Leonard's grandmother's. Laurie's sense of personal security was affected as homicide detectives sat in her home in the middle of the night telling her that her sister-in-law was dead and that they were trying to find Christopher. They did find him later that morning, hidden from view, covered by laundry.

As I understand the events, Leonard had asked Pat for help and Pat had agreed. He stole her videos, including Christopher's special Michael Jackson and Elton John videos. Sometime after Loretta left to return to Largo that Sunday, he killed both of them.

He used her car and sold anything and everything of any value. He sold all her videos. He sold *Bambi, The Lion King, The Wizard of Oz*, another VCR, the TV, Christopher's Whiz Kid computer and his Mickey Mouse radio, and the dinnerware and glassware that I gave her for Christmas that were still in the boxes because they were for the new apartment.

These things I bought back from the pawnshop. Her secondhand computer that she was so proud of, I've never found.

He used her home to call for taxis and pizzas, to frighten working people, and to steal a few dollars, all while Pat and Christopher lay dead nearby.

He used her car to go to pawnshops, to rob people in parking lots, and to buy drugs. He used her phone to make a thousand dollars' worth of calls.

All for crack cocaine!

I am a nurse and have worked most of the last twenty years in addictions. I've worked in Manatee and Sarasota. I've interviewed people in the jail across the street. I've accompanied clients to appearances in the old courthouse. I've seen enough to know that addiction is powerful. I also know that recovery is possible.

Chapter 5 of the "Big Book" of Alcoholics Anonymous states, "Rarely have we seen a person fail who has thoroughly followed our path. Those who do not recover are people who cannot or will not completely give themselves to this simple program, usually men and women who are constitutionally incapable of being honest with themselves."

Today I will roar like an angry lion. I will let my rage out into the universe in ways that are totally harmonious for everyone concerned.

Edna St. Vincent Millay said, "Childhood is the place where nobody dies." But we don't live in the world of children anymore. Why is that? And why should our childhoods be over already? Who said? Why?

There is a part of us that needs to rage; sometimes, we could take a few cues from children. They pound their fists, yell, and scream at injustice. God bless my anger and grief. Fill my eyes with healing tears of rage.

But I am afraid to be angry. Rage betrays the need to accept what has happened. Yet I am more afraid to accept. Acquiescence might suggest that I have given in to injustice. Despite the taboo on anger, I sense that I have that right, even though it will not alter the facts. It is not *I understand but am furious*; it is *I understand* and *am furious*.

I am also grateful that I have a deep, although undefined, relationship with a higher power. It has helped me make it through some of the darkest days.

Small children have an openness that often escapes us as we get older. Ms. Young's kindergarten class at Phillippi Shores School wrote this:

We learned some news at school
It made us very sad
After lots of tears and talking
We went home to Mom and Dad
We gathered round the counselor
   All seated on the rug
We heard what happened to our friend
   Some kids needed a hug
Brown hair and a big happy smile
   We're going to miss that little guy
But when he didn't get his way
   He would sit right down and cry
This happened a lot so ...
   Our teacher taught us what to do
It wasn't hard to fix
   We just brought him a tissue or two.
He was a good helper and a best friend
   When it came to blocks and tricky puzzles
He had a hand to lend
He loved to eat his snack
   And would politely ask for more
He kept his snack calendar at home
On the refrigerator door
   On the playground ...
   He loved to swing and run with speed
In the classroom ...
   He was just attempting to write stories and read
If you asked him his name
   A nickname he didn't need
He would answer so proud
My name is Christopher Thomas Reed
We learned about past memories
   And good times to plan and share
We learned that Christopher's life was cut short by violence
   And this is just not fair

My friend Rev. William Hull of Kirkwood Presbyterian Church in Bradenton shared this affirmation during a service for Pat and Christopher:

"In the death of Jesus Christ, God's way in the world seemed finally defeated. But death was no match for God. The resurrection of Jesus was God's victory over death.

Death often seems to prove that life is not worth living, that our best efforts and deepest affections go for nothing. We do not yet see the end of death, but Christ has been raised from the dead, transformed, and is yet the same person.

In his resurrection is the promise of ours. We are convinced that the life that God wills for us is stronger than the death that destroys us. The glory of that life exceeds our imagination, but we know that we will be with Christ.

So we treat death as a broken power. Its ultimate defeat is certain. In the face of death we grieve. Yet in hope we celebrate life.

No life ends so tragically that its meaning and value are destroyed. Nothing, not even death, can separate us from the love of Jesus Christ, our Lord."

Although some are still conflicted about the death penalty, I believe that Pat's philosophy would be in agreement with the events of today and that she may have touched Leonard's heart to plead as he did.

I will close with Micah 6:8:

He has told you, O mortal, what is good;
and what does the Lord require of you
but to do justice, and to love kindness,
and to walk humbly with your God?

Memory

Sometimes I wonder about the strangeness of memory, why some things are so vivid and others diffuse. Often, the intensity of the memory doesn't equal the significance of the event. Sometimes I have to dig deeper and deeper to find the bits and pieces—fragments, really—of events that have most affected me in the core of my being.

Am I in danger of forgetting?

Other times, an irrelevant memory will slide out of the inner sanctum of my mind, complete, succinct, and in color.

Sometimes I wonder how memories, thoughts, and feelings collide and perhaps energize, illuminate, or create a new truth.

February 28, 2006

How I Became My Father

"Where are you going?" my father asked, stepping out of his black GTO as I approached the Mission, a halfway house my mother forced me into after bailing me out of jail.

"To get my things," I said.

"You know you can't leave. Your mother'll rescind your bail."

"Well, I can't stay here."

"Why not?"

"Never mind, man. I just can't."

We were facing each other before the ramshackle mission with its toddler-sized wooden cross hanging by a steel chain from the middle of the porch ceiling. Dope boys haunting the top of the block shouted the different colors of the caps on crack vials they were peddling while junkies slipped sweaty wads of cash into their palms.

My father looked away from me, ignored the dope boys, shaded his eyes with his hand, and stared at the Mission—a mud-brown monstrosity at the top of a block of row houses in Northwest Baltimore.

He looked at me. "Wanna go for a ride?"

I shrugged my shoulders and followed him to his car.

We drove around the city some before he parked beneath an old maple by the reservoir in the heart of Druid Hill Park.

"So," he said as I watched sunlight dance on the reservoir's slate-gray surface, "you want to tell me what's going on?"

I didn't. It would really have screwed with his head if I had told him. Might spill him right off the edge of sobriety into the hell it had taken him twenty years to climb out of.

"Nah, man," I said. "It'd be bad for you."

"Look, lil' Lenny," he said, "I haven't always been there for you."

He looked off and then turned back. "But I'm here now. And I'm your father. You can talk to me."

My favorite scene in the Star Wars trilogy is the one in *The Empire Strikes Back* where Darth Vader breaks Luke's heart with these four words: "I am your father."

I could dig Luke's terror and rage snarling in the "No!" he screamed before slipping and falling off the space station into the darkness below. You grow up without a dad, and you dream his ghost into a god. When Luke's phantom god was smashed and broken across Vader's confession, he lost his grip. If Vader was his father, what did it mean for *his* fate? The sins of the father, after all, are visited upon the son.

Unlike Luke, I'd known all along that my father was Vader. My mother had made it clear to me that my father was a crackhead. And that he was an asshole. And that he'd been in and out of prison—a bad guy. But I'd always secretly wished he were Obi-Wan Kenobi, something far more than he could ever be.

I looked at him and studied the intensity in his dark eyes. He frowned and nodded his head as if to say, *I'm telling the truth; you can believe me.* And I wanted to—because he was my father. And if you can't believe in your father, who can you believe in?

So I told him. And he turned away from me.

"I don't believe you," he said.

"You think I would lie about something like that?"

"You don't want to stay at the Mission," he said. "You make this crap up to justify leaving so your mother won't have you thrown back in jail."

He could have done a lot less damage by busting my lip and spitting in my face.

When my little sister, Erica, was six, she told my mother that Armando, my mother's boyfriend, had touched her vagina and kissed her.

My little brother, Andre, and I liked Armando. He wouldn't let our mother whip us. That made him a saint as far as we were concerned. And he told wild stories about banditos and Mexican ghosts after smoking a joint. He was a kick to have around. Believing Erica was not convenient for me, so I didn't.

"Momma's going to kick him out for that shit, Erica," I said. "You gotta tell the truth."

"I *am* telling the truth."

"I don't believe you."

I remembered Erica's eyes as I stared down the gullet of my father's convenient disbelief and felt ashamed. Maybe my father read it as shame from having told a terrible lie, but it wasn't. It was shame rising from having done to Erica what my father was doing to me.

I was sixteen when I first met my father.

Well, that may not be entirely accurate. I'd seen him once, twice, maybe, before then. I can't be absolutely certain about it. The first time was at one of my youth basketball games. I was nine.

I saw him sitting on the bleachers in the midst of a crowd of parents. My mother had mentioned that he might show up so, as I was riding the bench with the rest of the scrubs, I scanned the bleacher crowd for a glimpse of him.

I didn't know what he would look like. The only memory I had of him involved his penis—him standing before a urinal with his swipe in his hand as he instructed me on the finer points of pissing into a toilet bowl rather than on the floor. I had to have been two, maybe three.

At nine, I couldn't remember his face. So when this slim brown cat in a black fedora, gray trench coat, and dungarees waved to me from the crowd, the feeling of my lungs being clenched in a fist led me to believe it was him.

I wanted to impress this stranger so that he'd like me—because, if he liked me, he might want to hang out sometime. I begged Coach Murray to let me off the bench so my dad could see me play. But Coach wasn't having it. He wanted to win, he said. *So sit down and shut up.*

I did. Every so often, I'd look behind me into the crowd to see if the stranger I thought was my dad was still there. He'd wave his black fedora and smile. Once I tossed up a hand but was so tangled up inside about having to ride the bench that I quickly put both my hand and my head down.

Of course, tears were splashing against hardwood by the game's end. They coursed down my brown face like raindrops carving silver trails down a Chevy's cracked windshield as the other kids and their parents began filing out of the gym.

After a while, I looked up for my father, hoping he'd pick me up, hug me a little too roughly, and tell me to stop whining because it's only a game. We'd shoot a few hoops just before they locked the gym up, and he'd tell me the reason he hadn't been around was because he had a crime-fighting alter ego and didn't want his enemies to get wise to his family. He was protecting us, you see.

But I couldn't find him. I scanned the crowd moving across the hardwood gymnasium floor and out its double doors. But I couldn't spot the black fedora atop the tall, slim, brown man's head.

Andre sat beside me on the bench and asked me who I was looking for.

"Didn't you see Daddy?" I asked, wiping the tears from my face with my yellow jersey.

"Who?"

"Daddy, man. In the bleachers."

He frowned and looked at me as if I'd asked him if he'd seen Freddy Krueger walking up our block, clicking his quicksilver finger knives together.

"You okay?" he asked.

"What you mean?"

"I'm just askin'. You talking crazy right now."

"Why you say that?" I asked.

"'Cause you talking like Lenny's gonna come see you play basketball, and you can't even play basketball."

"Well ..."

"And he's probably smoking crack somewhere, anyway."

He was right. Maybe it hadn't been him. Maybe that guy in the fedora had been some other kid's dad and was waving to him.

I wouldn't see my father and know for certain it was him until the Christmas Day many years later that he took a day pass from the drug treatment center he was in to visit me and Andre at my mother's house.

Andre didn't seem to care about seeing Lenny as we waited for him, but this was huge for me. I wanted to know who this cat calling himself my father was. Like most sixteen-year-olds, I was having serious existential issues. There were no examples of manhood in my life other than the dope fiends around the way and the crackhead uncles I had. I found myself grappling alone with conflicting ideas about what it meant to be a young black man in America.

This was serious business for black boys of my generation: Generation X. In the absence of our fathers, we turned to the streets, to rap music and gangster movies, to define for us what black manhood was.

Who was harder than Nino Brown, cooler than Big Daddy Kane, sharper than the cat pushing an Acura Legend down the block as he clocked the boys who were hustling the crack he served them? "Get money, stay strapped, fuck the world" was the code every kid in the 'hood latched onto in his drive to survive. It was the gangster who epitomized manhood for us. Tony Montana. Don Corleone. John Gotti. Frank Lucas. The doctor was a square, the lawyer a shyster, the teacher a sucka. Only the gangster stood with his self-respect intact as he flipped the establishment the bird, his hand on his bozack like it weighed three tons.

None of that made sense to me. Knowing how to cook crack or load a gun wasn't cool to me; it was the work of a traitor who preyed upon his people. But there weren't any men around to guide me through the minefield of bullshit I was crawling through. All I had were my books: *The Destruction of Black Civilization, Manchild in the Promised Land, Soul on Ice, Soledad Brother.* But none of these books could answer the questions that plagued me so violently: *What is a man? How do I become one?*

I waited for my father in my mother's living room. Maybe he could give me the answers I was seeking.

I stopped breathing when he pulled up in a black 280 ZX, the sun glistening white on its hood. There'd been so many times in my young life that I'd prayed my father would pop up some night outside my window and take me away, times I'd hated him for staying gone, times I'd loved him so powerfully in his absence that I'd felt my heart would crack from the strain of it. All of this crystallized diamond hard and hot in my chest as I watched him step out of his car.

I measured him against myself. He was long and lean like me and moved with the smooth, wary steps of an alley cat.

"He's here," I announced.

My grandmother, mother, and sister grew quiet and stared as I walked to the door and opened it.

"Y'all ready?" this stranger asked without so much as a *Hey, how y'all doing? I'm your father.*

I studied his face for traces of myself. It was the first time in my life I could remember seeing the man who'd fathered me, and I was shocked by how much of my face I saw in his.

"Man, you look just like your daddy," my stepfather, who'd become friends with Lenny when they were in prison, had often said. But it had never occurred to me that he wasn't saying that just because it was a nice thing to say. My father and I had the same funny-looking mouth and angular nose, the same smooth and precise diction, the same liquid way of moving.

Andre and I followed him to his car. I sat in the front. Andre, sullen and silent, sat in the back.

I was quite astonished. After a lifetime of telling myself I'd never be like my crackhead father, looking at him was like looking in a mirror that projected twenty years into the future. He was me. I was him. And I didn't know how to feel about that.

We drove around for a little while. He didn't say anything that mattered. He had no keys to life, no cryptic answers to the great existential questions. There was no mention of his years of absence, of the woman he'd left us and my mother for, or of his dereliction or crack addiction.

"I'm saved," was all he had to say. He was a born-again Christian ordained as a reverend by a pastor who ran a mission for troubled men in the city.

Then he dropped us off at my mother's house, promising to see us again soon. I was spooked by the experience—by how similar our cadences were, our smiles, and our devils.

"I look just like him, don't I?" I asked my mother.

She stared at me through slitted eyes for a moment. "Doesn't mean you have to be like him," she said.

Dangling from the ceiling above a murky pool dug into the basement of a church one of Pastor Tim's colleagues presided over, a rough-hewn cross as tall as I was seemed a mere instant from crashing down to crack the pastor's skull open. He was standing waist-deep in the middle of the pool preaching the baptism—*Oh, hallelujah, Father God. Wash our sins away, Jehovah Jireh, for we are filthy with sin in your sight, Lord.*

And I was waiting to see blood.

So focused was I on waiting to see the old cross fall down and spill the pastor's brains into the gray pool that I didn't hear him call my name. I would have continued staring at the cross and its thick iron chain bolting it to the ceiling if my father hadn't nudged my shoulder.

"It's all right, son," he said. "You don't have to be afraid. Jesus loves you."

Pastor called me again.

I wasn't at all thrilled about being baptized. I'd already been baptized half a dozen times in my life, and it had never done anything for me beyond getting me soaked. It did not save me. I did not see Jesus beneath the waters. My father, however, was really psyched about the whole deal, so, not wanting to disappoint him, I stepped toward the pool's edge, climbed down the short aluminum ladder, and slipped into the frigid water.

"Praise Gawd," George or one of the other five men from the Mission gathered around the pool cried as I waded toward Pastor. A distinguished-looking man with a silver-streaked Afro, Pastor smiled his benevolent smile; pushed his gold, wire-rimmed glasses up his narrow nose; and placed his hand on top of my head when I reached him. "In the name of the Father, Son, and Holy Ghost, I—"

The rest of what he said was lost to me when, without warning, he shoved me beneath the cold water's surface. I should have anticipated it, but I hadn't, and being so abruptly dunked jacked my heartbeat as intensely as snorting a rail of coke would have. Grabbing Pastor's wrist with both hands, I opened my eyes and saw nothing. It was as if I'd been shoved down into some Antarctic hell.

After a few seconds that spanned into eternity, I was raised up into Pastor's embrace, gasping as he whispered, "I'm so proud of you, Leonard."

His lips grazed my ear. The Mission brothers on the edge of the pool harmonized *Amazing Grace*.

"You are cleansed," Pastor said.

I was cold. My teeth were chattering. My heart was spazzing. I didn't feel cleansed. I didn't feel any different at all. I was still me. My sojourn into that Antarctic hell had no other impact beyond instilling in me the firm conviction that I'd never again volunteer for the experience.

Lenny was waiting for me when I made it to the pool's edge. He extended his hand and clasped my arm as I climbed out of the pool.

There were tears in his eyes.

I crept out one of the Mission's third-story windows later that evening, climbed down the fire escape's black steel ladder, and didn't take a full breath until I was safe in the alley behind the Mission. If Pastor or any of the Mission guys woke up and spotted me, they'd call Mom and I'd be in some serious shit. She'd bailed me out of jail on the condition that I live in the Mission, turn my life around, and see the light of Jesus—praise Gawd—while awaiting trial on an assault charge. If she found out I was creeping, my black ass was going back to jail.

But I didn't care. The whole thing with the constant prayer, Narcotics Anonymous, and ice-cold baptisms wasn't doing it for me. It wasn't anywhere near as bad as getting beat down by twenty-seven Bloods in a Baltimore City Detention Center dormitory, and I would have eaten dingle berries out of a wino's butt if that had been a condition of getting bailed out of that hellhole, but the square thing was a drag. I had to get out into the real world before I choked on a Bible, so I crept into my beloved city.

This is the thing about Baltimore: sometimes you can look into the black sky pocked white with starlight and imagine for a moment that the city doesn't rage beneath your feet. But that sense of peace doesn't last. The city won't let you forget that she owns you. Her alleys are veins, and you're the lifeblood flowing into the streets that are her arteries, carrying you through her decaying body.

She is the undead, rotten with plague. If you are not diseased before you enter her, she will infect you before you leave.

But I loved the sickness, even found freedom in it. I took a deep, mildew stained breath in the dark alley, walked through it, slid onto the streets, and followed my normal route past the gangstas hunkered down in shadows blowing silver mist into their frozen palms. I was startled by the moon propped plump and marble above the roofs of Baltimore's crumbling brownstones and row houses as I moved deeper into my beloved.

My city was a whore wasted on crack, heroin, and pain. I'd always had a fascination with them—whores. They sell what I consider to be a priceless, sacred commodity for pennies. They are beautiful in their degradation, like the Black Madonna: nappy haired with bared breasts, lipstick smeared across her mouth, and bruises beneath her eyes as she seeks sanctuary in the arms of another lover.

My Madonna that night wore a maroon dress with its hem fraying along the contour of her thighs. She stood beneath a streetlamp, her hand on her cocked hip as she watched me approach. She smiled when I got close enough to appreciate it, licked her African lips, and asked if I had a cigarette.

I stopped for her eyes. Their whites were as pale and luminescent as the sullen moon above us. I reached into my pocket and slipped a Newport from my pack, and she touched my hand. Her fingernails were chipped and half-polished in scarlet.

I struck my lighter, and she cupped my hand in her palms, smiling as she leaned toward the flame. Smoke streamed between us a moment as she watched me and exhaled. She smiled some more and licked her lips.

"You been looking for me, haven't you?" she asked.

"How much?"

"For you—ten dollars. You're cute."

We walked then.

"What you doin' out here?" she asked. "You don't look the type."

"I'm not."

I didn't ask her name. She would have lied anyway. We found a bench and sat down, surrounded by a cluster of row houses, their windows boarded up with rotted plywood. The shabby buildings stood around us like blocky, gapped-toothed winos on the verge of toppling over at any moment. Crack vials, white dust caked in their bottoms, scattered sparks of moonlight at our feet.

Jezebel propped her purse on her lap and removed from it a piece of hollow car antenna, its end stuffed with steel wool.

"Hold this," she said, handing the crack pipe to me.

She took a small, blue-capped glass vial of crack out of her purse and then snatched the pipe back.

I'd always wondered what power lived in those stones. My father had murdered twenty years of his life for the love of them. I'd watched friends get the meat dragged off their bones, their souls shredded on hard streets in their chase of the rock.

Once I stood ankle-deep in dirty snow on a street off North Avenue, immersed in pitch-black night while my favorite aunt, Diane, scampered through the dark to cop some base. I'd thought she'd dragged me through the snow to buy some weed, but the telltale sizzle of the burning crack slipping from beneath her bedroom door after we got back to her house betrayed her.

I hadn't known she was a crackhead. The revelation was nothing short of walking into a room and finding one of your closest friends with a little boy's penis in his mouth.

Jezebel opened the vial and tapped a rock into her pipe.

"Let me hold your lighter," she said.

I gave it to her. She struck it. The flame's blue-orange light danced against her chocolate skin. She sucked the fire into her pipe. The crack hissed, and the flame died. She closed her eyes, held the smoke, and shuddered.

After a few moments, she blew a thin stream of sickeningly sweet smoke through her pursed lips.

"Want some?" she asked when she came back.

I'd seen what the shit had done to my father. I'd seen the havoc it had wrought in people's lives. It was an animal that ripped into a man or woman with its gnashing teeth and wouldn't let go until there was nothing left but blood and bone.

She handed me the pipe. It was warm. She tapped another rock into its mouth, and I slipped the broken antenna between my lips. I positioned my lighter, lit the fire, and inhaled.

A white, electric flower bloomed in my belly. In that incandescent moment, I felt closer to God than I'd ever felt during any prayer or baptism.

Jezebel got down on her knees. I held the smoke in. She unzipped my fly, and I closed my eyes.

I was lost.

Pastor called my name from the darkness behind me as I walked across a basketball court a block away from the Mission. I turned and saw him jogging after me, the hem of his burgundy robe flapping around his bare shins.

I stopped. I don't know why. Maybe I wanted to hear something more than, "My bad; it was a misunderstanding. I didn't mean to have my hands on your balls."

This man had been my mentor for a time, my father's mentor, and the first real connection to my father I'd ever had. How many times had we sat at a table in Lexington Market eating chicken wings slathered in hot sauce and ketchup, drinking Cokes while rapping about fatherhood, transcending limitations, forgiveness, and what it takes to be a good man? How many times had he fed me the lines about Christ being the paragon for manhood and leadership and that to be more than what my father had been I'd need to turn on to Christ, get saved, and find redemption in his blood?

I'd never really bought much of it, but there'd been moments during which I'd suspended my natural skepticism. Some well-guarded part of me wanted to forgive enough to believe that I could be saved—from myself, from my life—and that Pastor could show me the way.

I should have kept moving, kept it all behind me, and faced the cold ahead untainted by hypocrisy, but I stopped. And waited. And when he reached me, he handed me a twenty-dollar bill, shoved his glasses up his nose, and said, "We'll keep this between me and you. I'll make sure your mother doesn't send you back to jail."

I turned away without responding and slipped the twenty into my pocket. I walked several blocks and bought four nickel rocks of crack. I found an abandoned garage and sought solace in the cocaine's sweet, electric smoke, the same solace I imagine my father had often sought.

It was in this moment that I began to understand why he'd been a ghost for much of my life.

As I sat beside my father, facing Pastor in chairs set up in the Mission's chapel, I felt him on the verge of an upheaval, the earth tilting beneath his feet. Slowly clenching and unclenching his fists on top of his thighs, Lenny waited for me to repeat the sordid tale I'd told him in his car.

I shouldn't have told him. I'd known going in that it would screw with his head but had been seduced by the thought that he was my father and would understand and help me make sense of Pastor's betrayal, but it still bit one. That was a mistake. He was Christian to the bone. His faith was his foundation, was what had saved him. Having it stripped from his grasp without prelude or preamble could be nothing less than devastating for him. I could understand his need to not believe me.

Pastor sat across from me, avoiding my gaze. A dark, fat vein snaking across his right temple pulsed so quickly and violently that it seemed ready to burst and splash us all with his sinner's blood. His intermittent attempts to smile and appear pastorally with his white cleric's collar that should've been burning a hole through his throat would have made me laugh if I hadn't been so tethered to my own hurt.

That he could sit before me and my father wearing his preacher's costume in the chapel, ready to spill a Bible verse or two from his lips, affirmed my years long suspicion that the Jesus trip was bunk. I mean, Pastor was Christ's representative on earth, right? The man who'd ordained men like my father, setting them on fire for the Lord; the man who'd baptized me, who'd ministered to me; the man who'd pulled my father out of the gutter and set him on two feet with a Bible in his hand instead of a pipe was the same guy who only hours before had given me twenty dollars to keep quiet about his fondling my genitals while I was asleep. Didn't do much for Jesus's image, in my mind.

"Well, what's this about?" Pastor asked.

"My son has something to say to you."

I looked at my father. He wasn't meeting my eyes either. Maybe he was ashamed of me—or of himself. I didn't know. But the onus to expose his mentor for the douche bag that he was was on me.

Could my father handle that? With barely a year clean after twenty years of crack love, did my father have the required moxie to resist relapse after I pointed out the pitchfork the Pastor had shoved into his spine?

On the other hand, so what if he couldn't? He was grown. And I didn't owe him jack; he owed me, for all the years I needed him while he was running the streets chasing crack; for all the things he should have taught me but hadn't; for all the footballs never tossed, the answers never given, and the love never shared. I owed him jack, zilch, nothin'. He'd never been any more than a stranger to me, even now.

Still … yet and still. He was my father. And in spite of everything, he meant something to me.

"I lied to my father, Pastor," I said. "And told him …"

"Oh—that, Brother Leonard," he interrupted, smiling his first genuine smile of the day. "We've already discussed that. He's apologized and, really, there's no harm done."

There had been a small, insistent hope within me that, in the end, Pastor would affirm the fragile faith I'd once had in him and prove himself to be a better man than he actually was, that he wouldn't leave me a liar in my father's eyes but would man up and take the burden on his shoulders.

But he didn't.

He lied right along with me.

Never mind that Pastor and I hadn't had an opportunity to speak between this meeting and the moment I'd told Lenny that his pastor was a freak, my father clung to that lie for dear life. And he suggested that we pray so that Gawd, have mercy, would forgive me my sin. So we prayed. And I couldn't hear all the words. I was too busy contending with the earth tilting beneath my feet, spilling me over the edge.

Shattered Reality

I remember a room, a small office, in 1998. Two male, uniformed officers and me at perhaps two or three a.m.

Not so very unusual except that they hadn't come to see me to bring someone for admission or to respond to a disturbance.

I had been apprehensive throughout the evening, trying to reach my daughter in another city.

Now these officers had a small card with a number to call. I made the call while they stood by.

The man on the other end asked if there was an officer present and if he could speak with him.

The face of the officer with the phone in his hand confirmed that the news was bad.

He silently handed the phone back to me. I remained standing with the phone to my ear.

The two officers huddled, talking in hushed tones to each other.

The disembodied voice on the other end of the phone recited the news he was assigned to tell.

Whatever vague apprehensions, even fear, I had did not come close to the reality of his words.

Still I remember only fragments. Someone said we remember moments, not days.

Sometimes a moment is an eternity.

Pat and Christopher, both dead. Incomprehensible!

Murdered! I can hear no more.

Hand out of blue coat takes the phone from me ...

March 13, 2003

Leonard

If you want to know if I've suffered for what I've done, I have. That should be argument enough against the death penalty. We can't know for certain if someone who has killed goes to hell after they are executed, but we can be certain that the person serving a life sentence in prison is living in hell.

Solitude

These bars cut the sun into black strips of shadows that claw these walls,
flay the soul, hammer the mind to pulp.

All these grave hours of jagged shadows crush the heart;
and it stinks: the spine bruised by the concrete slab I shiver upon,
the kinked neck, shrunken belly, nails gnawed to the quick;
the red-rimmed eyes staring at the criss-cross patchwork of shadows
battering these walls.
No one's eyes can hide me from myself here.
There is no music to soothe my savage beast.
My delusions crumble like old leaves in winter.

I take the pen and carve tears into white pages,
running from shadows, delving into reflection, puking my sins
into the light of day.

I take the pen.

And scream.

2003

Solitude

The word *solitude* has so many meanings and implications: isolation, loneliness, aloneness; short-term solitude, long-term, chosen, imposed, silent, joyous, frightening, warm, cold.

Solitude, for me, means a quiet beach walk at sunrise or sunset, reflection, marveling at the wonders of the universe, or listening to music in a soft light; crawling under the covers on a cold, rainy Saturday afternoon; reading a good book; or walking around the block before sunrise.

Solitude also means aloneness and sometimes loneliness. It is a reminder of those who have gone before. As a daughter, my parents are gone; as a sister, my sister is gone; as a parent, my children are gone; as a grandparent, my grandson is gone.

Solitude reminds me of the hole in the floor of heaven, and they are all looking down.

March 1999

I Wasn't Ready

My oldest child, my daughter, Pat Reed, entered residential treatment for a long dependency on alcohol. I was ready.

My youngest grandson, Christopher Reed, came to live with me while his mother was in treatment. He was four. I wasn't ready.

We learned, he and I, preschool, music, reading, transportation, packing lunches, running, playing ball, quiet time, time-out. We became ready.

Pat completed treatment, embraced sobriety, and again became able to care for herself and Christopher. After eighteen months, he returned to live with his mom. I was almost ready.

A year later, she mentioned plans to help a young man on his way toward recovery from crack cocaine. I urged caution. She said, "You always said everyone deserves a chance." I wasn't ready.

I tried to reach her by phone without success. She didn't go to work. Her employer was concerned. It was very unlike her. After I called the police, they went to Pat's apartment. It was a Thursday night, and I was working when two officers came to where I was. I wasn't ready.

When the lieutenant told me, "Pat and Christopher are both dead"— she was forty years old, he was six—I wasn't ready.

When he told me they had been murdered, I wasn't ready.

When he told me they had been killed by Leonard, the twenty-one-year-old young man she was trying to help, I wasn't ready.

When the victim advocate came to see me and I tried to believe this unreal reality, I wasn't ready.

The detective told me on the phone that Leonard was in custody and that he had confessed. I wasn't ready.

This was a person with whom Pat had attempted to share the gift of sobriety. This was a person I had met when he was nineteen. I wasn't ready.

When I went to the morgue, I wasn't ready.

When I spoke with her husband and her older children, I wasn't ready.

When I spoke with family, friends, and colleagues; Pat's coworkers and her recovery community; Christopher's teacher and classmates, I wasn't ready.

When memorial services were held, the love and care of so many friends were warmly welcomed, but I wasn't ready.

I've chosen to honor my children by trying to live the words "everyone deserves a chance" without ever forgetting that they must also be accountable.

Years have passed since that horrific time, and I still am not ready.

April 2000

Drum

I hear a drum echoing heartbeat.
More often I hear a different drummer,
different from others and different than yesterday,
incessant, yet I can hush that drum.
Listen and march with feet solid on the ground.
Listen and tiptoe around, skipping lightly.
Listen, lying still, trying to follow a new rhythm.
The drum, the heartbeat, the conductor, the writer, the unknown becoming familiar.
The drum is always there.
The listening is the choice.

On Bursting Bubbles of Light

Nietzsche's mind splintered
when he saw a man beating a horse.
He lost it; never returned.
Tuned in to Buddha, perhaps, who lost it too
beneath the Bodhi tree when he dissolved
in a star burning in the black sky above him.

We are everything hit him hard as young love
and he felt himself burning in the infinite, cold
sea of dark energy, the earth in his throat,
Orion an anklet of diamonds, the Pleiades
a bracelet of white fire around his wrist.

We are everything, even horses beaten
with skinny leather whips. And Nietzsche dissolved
when he felt that leather tear into his bruised flanks
and the wild-eyed, sweaty terror and sting tore him
from the *dream,* assaulted him with boundless compassion
so abrupt and heavy it cracked the vessel.

Unlike Gautama, Nietzsche didn't return to us with any noble truths.
He stayed silent, gone, immersed in the maelstrom of light.

In the End

In the end, we are touched and shaped by each other. In the end, each of those who have passed through my time and space have been part of the creation that is me. Some I've known very well; some I thought I knew; others I've not known at all.

My parents, with all our conflicts; my free-spirited sister, who joined and left the convent; my nature-loving brother with the unseen sadness; the men I married and the ones I didn't; my children, with their struggles for independence—all have shaped me.

Good times, not so good times, and those that were unbearable, yet endurable, in the end.

Teachers, mentors, healers, ministers of many professions or none. A word, a thought, a song, a touch—all are now part of my being.

Students, hurting souls, seekers, those at the end of life and those with vast horizons. Those sharing joys, hurts and sorrows, shattered dreams, and unexpected peace.

I'm all of those I've met on subways; in diners at three a.m.; in hospitals, busy offices, classrooms, and prisons; in grocery stores and banks, gas stations and airports; in hotels and living rooms; and in words put on paper by those I'll never meet.

In the end, I am them, and I leave a bit of me with each of them.

December 4, 2008

Perspectives on Crime and Victimization

Two things changed my mind on crime and victimization. The first was my brother Andre's death in 2005. Until the moment my grandmother told me in a prison visitation room that Andre was gone, I had no true emotional connection to the soul shredding that the victims of my own crimes had suffered.

I'd been remorseful about my crimes and had felt a tremendous amount of guilt, but I hadn't the beginning of a clue about what that phone call from a Sarasota detective informing Agnes of Pat and Chris's murders had been like for her: the moment of disbelief, the confusion and sense of dislocation, reality's dawning, and the collapse of something within the chest, a chasm opening—a black hole whose gravity is so intense that it sucks away all light, hope, laughter, and joy, leaving nothing but desolation in its wake. I came to know it all quite intimately.

Holding my grandmother's hand as we wept, my handcuffs biting into my wrists as a white dwarf star exploded in my viscera, I knew then that I could never be redeemed. Andre was my brother, not a life brought through my flesh into this world. How much more devastating were Pat and Chris's murders to those who loved them? Was I truly responsible for creating pain like this in their lives after having stolen Pat and Chris's? How much of a monster—an animal—did that make me?

In the months that followed, my grief was compounded by the knowledge that I'd created that pain in the lives of people whose names I didn't know but whose hurt I could now identify with. When I wept for my little brother, clinging to the memories I had of him; when I'd shove my face into my pillow so other convicts couldn't hear me breaking down after reading letters he'd written just before his passing; when I'd come to the daily realization that my little brother was no longer walking the earth with me and would feel the black hole blooming in my chest, I understood it as karma, as the return to me of what I had created in the hearts and souls of others.

It was in this state that Agnes found me.

"The world is much more interconnected than the old physics let on."
—John Bell

I wish I still had Agnes's letters from the first couple of years of our correspondence. Unfortunately, they were thrown away by Department of Corrections staff when I was transferred from Florida State Prison in 2005. It would've been great to partner her letters with mine so that we could share with you the back and forth we experienced as our journey evolved.

Since we don't have those letters, we've done the next best thing by choosing poems that Agnes wrote during those first years of our journey. Each poem has a relationship with the period of time within which we took those first bold steps.

Listening to Pen on Paper

I find myself on paper with my pen as my compass. When I'm lost, my pen touches paper and shows me direction, a map into my being.

My pen is my cartographer, the paper my topography.

My pen often goes down roads I hadn't planned, that perhaps I hadn't known were there.

I find myself exploring scary terrain, jumping off cliffs, edges, and into thin spaces.

January 24, 2006

January 7, 2005

Agnes,

This is my first reaction to your card: surprise. I certainly wasn't expecting to receive such a mysterious note.

Please forgive my ignorance, Agnes, but I don't have anyone or know anyone in Florida, so I am at a loss as to why you would've been thinking about me over the years. (I'm from Baltimore.)

I can see that you are a woman of taste and style. This is a very cute card, and it gets extra points in my book for being produced on paper recycled by a company that's earth friendly. So I'm thinking that I should know a woman who pays attention to these sorts of things, but I can't connect a face to your name and feel like a schmuck because of it.

And you've underlined the word *peace*, which is something I've searched for all my life. It has special significance for me. What significance does it have for you? What impulse moved you to underline it?

You said you hoped I am well. I am. I'm alive, and that is beautiful. These are difficult times I'm grappling with, but I try to find the joy within them. Saturday, I learned that my little brother, Andre, had passed away. I've been caught up in trying to come to terms with that. I don't know if I ever will, but I take comfort in the fact that there was nothing left unsaid between us. We didn't make that mistake. He knew how deeply I cared for him. And I know he cared for me just as deeply. What makes it so tough to deal with is that he had so many dreams he wanted to fulfill. So many goals, so many plans ... but I guess he moved on to a greater destiny. Wow, he was a beautiful kid.

I'm sorry; I don't want to depress you. I don't know why you've reached out to me during such a wild time, but I'd like you to know it was a lovely gesture. It's given me something to smile about, and I thank you. But, Agnes, how are we connected? You've gotten through many of my defenses with this wonderful mystery you've introduced into my life. Here I am speaking to you of things I've kept buried while I've tried to keep my head above water.

Maybe I should stop talking. It's your turn. In what other ways have you tried to contact me?

Why has it been important to you to do so?

I've probably scared the bejeezus out of you with all this talk of what's going on with me right now, but I hope I haven't. You have got me interested in who *you* are. And I hope I haven't insulted you by not knowing.

So, Agnes, tell me—what's this all about?

Peace and blessings to you,
Leonard

When I got the response asking who I was, I was angry—maybe more than angry—and said so when I answered, "How can you not know who I am? You changed my life forever. You killed my daughter and grandson."

Somewhere along the Way

I began to believe
in the cloud of unknowing.

I began to understand that in our literate world
there are things that are unknowable.

October 2002

January 25, 2005

Agnes,

It is incredible that you've chosen to write to me. Please forgive me for not knowing who you were, but I never learned your name. I recall *you,* and I've thought about you often. When I was at my first prison camp, I'd tried to contact you, but the prison chaplain wouldn't allow it. I didn't know your name, of course, but I knew it wouldn't be at all difficult to find you.

Agnes, at times I am socially clumsy and inappropriate, so please forgive me for my tactlessness. But I must tell you that I have never and will never forget Pat or Chris, and I don't seek forgiveness for what I've done or the pain I've caused so many innocent people. So many lives were destroyed and irrevocably altered by my evil, senseless act, and I will continue to be sorry for and regretful of and haunted by it until I, myself, am dead.

I don't know the depth of the sorrow I've caused; I can only imagine it. I was a very, very sick young man. So sick. At the time, I was lost to drugs, guilt, rage, and pain and ... I punished Pat for daring to love me. That's how I've seen things in retrospect. She did not deserve what I did to her, and Chris certainly didn't. Pat was truly one of the sweetest, most generous, honest, and loving people I've known. And Chris was unblemished and ... I realize saying I'm sorry doesn't cut it.

Nothing ... words are weak in the face of all this. But I want you to know that whatever you require of me, whatever questions you need to ask, I am available to you.

My brother was twenty-six.

I'd hoped he'd escape some of the mistakes I'd made with my life. But he didn't. I'd hoped he'd look at me and see what he didn't want to become, but, as he always did when we were children, he decided to follow in my confused, bumbling footsteps, and instead of ending up in prison, he ended up dead.

I've felt him with me.

That is why I know some wounds can never heal; new flesh may cover them, but they still bleed deep inside. What do you need from me? Have you found closure? When I sought to speak with you, it was with the thought that perhaps facing me could bring some closure to the fallout from what I'd done to you and your family.

Is it in you to hate me? I definitely wouldn't blame you. But you've never seemed to have that kind of heart. Do you know what I remember most about seeing and hearing you in that courtroom? You said that when you met me, I frightened you. That has stayed with me. It got through the drugs I was medicated on at the time and sank its roots in my soul. I wanted to look at you, but one of the crap lawyers I had told me not to and I obeyed like a zombie. But I felt like I was cheating you of something because you never got the chance to confront me, to make me answer for my crimes. You never got your chance to make me know what you were feeling. You didn't even know that I cared and was broken by all of what I'd done.

You didn't even know if I was in pain or if I was living with it cavalierly.

I was and will forever be in pain. My soul is seared with the mark of my sins and the devastation it wrought in you and your family's lives. I don't seek forgiveness, and I've chosen not to forgive myself.

My life in prison has not been easy. I've experienced difficulty and tragedy since coming in. I'm only recently arriving at a place, mentally, where I've been able to take stock of my life and make serious changes … not that I haven't reflected on life the entire time I've been here. But I am only beginning to realize what it all means … and am realizing how little I've known all my life.

I'm glad you were courageous enough to write to me because I wanted to offer my soul to you. I've wondered how you and Chris's other grandmother have dealt with your pain. I've wanted you to have your chance to confront me and tell me and ask me all you need to ask.

What more is there to say at this point?

I am open to you completely. Whatever you want or need from me is yours.

I return your greeting of peace and hope my social awkwardness has not disturbed you.

> Peace and blessings to you, Ms. Furey,
> Leonard

Again

Standing
at the edge of the cliff,
at the top of the bridge,
invites terror.

A fluttering in the belly
when you fall
and run into darkness,
into clouds
of unknowing,

where messages again,
again, and again
challenge beliefs.

Ancestors, siblings, descendants
walked through the *thin space;*
but why do I still live?

Because the Universe has plans, I hear
as my life unfolds with meaning,
faith, joy, hope, wonder.

May 4, 2006

February 10, 2005

Agnes,

It was good to hear from you. But why do you, or would you, think I wouldn't want to hear from you? Any reasons I would have for harboring such a feeling would be selfish, childish. To the contrary, I look forward to hearing from you.

Why? Because I recognize this as an opportunity for healing to occur. That is why I don't think you've reached out to me to jab your finger in my face and scream invectives at me, though even if it were your reason, I would still offer you the chance to do just that. You must have been and still must be so angry with me. I'm angry with me. And ashamed. No, I approach this situation and you very humbly, knowing the gravity of all that has transpired.

How could you not be cynical? There is no need with me, though. I have no promises to make. I don't consciously seek anything besides some manner of healing. But this is more about you than about me. Your healing, or whatever else it is that you seek, takes precedence over anything concerning me.

When we met in '96, I was indeed using. It was the reason I left First Step. I fought against it but was not equipped to handle the power of my addiction.

You said you saw rage in me. It is still there. I live with it. Like many who are prone to addiction, I was beaten, kicked, spit on, raped, betrayed, abandoned, and terrorized as a child. I'm only now overcoming much of the damage I sustained during those times. Still there are scars. The rage was a direct product of my being so thoroughly abused as a child. Maturity has tempered it. I have more control over myself than I did when I was nineteen and twenty, but wounds, as you know, don't disappear.

In '96 I was so lost ... so lost and wild and confused and needful. Pat saw beyond that fire searing me inside to the soul of a man struggling to survive as he warred with himself. And I saw her, too; you have to understand. I saw this bright, courageous, incredibly loving, generous, awakening woman struggling against her own demons, and I did love her and was amazed by her love for and acceptance of me.

Of course I manipulated her, but not maliciously. I think many thought I was merely using Pat and cared nothing for her, which was so far from the truth as to be ridiculous. At that time I knew absolutely nothing about how to love. All I'd known up to that point was destruction. I knew little of what it meant to be alive. But, in my way, I loved her as best I could, which isn't saying much, because even then, I hurt and disappointed her. Then I ran back to Baltimore, leaving her alone.

I wasn't running from her. She was the sweetest thing, the sweetest experience and person I'd known here. I was running from my addiction. My brother, Andre, had hurt his leg very badly, and my grandfather paid my way back home. I'd hoped to be able to kick back at home—and for a while I did. I went to college, taught eleventh- and twelfth-grade English and social studies, got involved in the local arts scene, and generally did okay for a while. But my friend, the beast, dragged me into the dirt again—harder this time—and if I was lost before, I was forsaken then.

I sense that you want to understand what happened. I think that as you learn more and more, your sense of the tragedy of what has happened will deepen. Because, really, I think it would be easier for you if I were some unrepentant, unthinking, vitriolic monster. But I'm far from that, Agnes. I'm a man who loved your daughter, who victimized her, your grandson, and all of those who love Pat and Chris for no rational reason besides the fact that I was crazed on coke and ... besides that, there is nothing. Take the coke out of the equation, and we wouldn't be having this conversation; none of this would have happened because I could not have harmed Pat or Chris. Still coke is not a rational reason. There is no rational reason.

This is why I wear my shame like a tattoo. If those moments could have left a physical trace, I'd be a hunchbacked, crooked-spined, leprous man. I am so totally warped by what I have done to you all that it is difficult, near impossible, to look at myself as a whole man. I think of your pain and wonder how Pat's other children, whom I've never known, have dealt with their loss. I've thought of the havoc wrought by my actions and of Pat, whom I loved, and in memory love and of Chris, whom I didn't know, but … I wonder about justice. I don't believe in it, Agnes, not in this life. Because I should be dead—not Pat, not Chris, not my brother. But I am here, and I don't have the courage or fortitude to kill myself.

So, no, I certainly don't believe in justice.

Do you know that I did not attempt to conceal my crime and essentially led the police to myself? No, I didn't give myself up. I was not going to walk into a police station and give myself up, not while I was in the grip of that drug. But I did everything I possibly could to force the police to find me, hoping they'd shoot and kill me because I didn't have the strength to do it myself.

Did you really think I was a stupid, ignorant fool of a man who would have done all of those things afterward out of simple idiocy?

Agnes, I cannot tell you what thoughts swirled through my drug-addled mind when, afterward, I was alone in the house and acutely aware of what I'd done. Many people kill themselves immediately after they kill someone because when that ugly impulse that drove them over the edge is gone, they are left with the grave knowledge of what they have done. They have more courage than I do because they inflict their own punishment on themselves and put the pistol under their chins and pull the trigger.

That is their closure.

But, you are right—there is no closure for the living. It is never over, is it?

How have you changed?

You suggest that I may have changed. I'm older and, I hope, wiser. But I've never been a bad guy without the drugs. In fact, some have found reason to love me. I just hope I've gotten rid of some of the garbage I carried from my childhood. I hope that I have become a better man. It's hard for me to really judge because I'm incredibly hard on myself. That is for others to see and acknowledge in me.

If you want to sit down and talk with me, I'm available to you. In Europe it is a regular practice. The courts encourage it. I think we may find opposition here, though. But I think you may be after … truth? What is it that you seek?

I don't mean to imply that I don't get anything out of this. I've needed to talk with you. I have needed you to understand what it was all about and what it wasn't about. I've wanted to tell you I'm sorry, as weak as that is, you know. So I'm not saying there is nothing in it for me, but my primary thought is you. Your pain and grief are sacred, while mine are profane.

I hope to hear from you soon.

Peace and blessings to you,
Leonard

Wildflowers in the Median

I find myself staring at this clump of deep pink and red wildflowers. It reminds me of Christopher.

When we drove up and down the interstate every weekend, he was fascinated by the wildflowers growing in the median. He would call out the colors of each section. He especially liked the red ones.

We rode so much that noticing things on the roadside became a kind of ritual. We would see cows and horses, fences, flowers, and trees. He would squeal when we drove under an overpass.

The flowers, when they were in bloom, were a special treat. He was studying the rain forest, and he would say the flowers reminded him of it. He became an avid recycler.

Days after he was murdered, a friend visited. She handed me a bunch of wildflowers she had picked along the interstate. This was very out of character for her! She said something told her to do it.

We believe it was a little boy named Christopher.

Spring 2002

I attended a workshop within a year of the murders. The presenter, Dr. Ron Barrett, was a psychologist who worked with young people and gangs in Los Angeles. His message was that there is a relationship between young male violence and unresolved grief. There is no model for young men but to "man up." If a family member dies or a parent goes to prison, a neighbor, peer, or sibling gets shot or overdoses and dies, no emotional response is expected or tolerated.

At the end of his talk, Dr. Barrett put a picture of a happy baby on the screen and quietly said, "They all start out that way."

We don't get to choose our roads, only how we walk them.

Leonard

March 10, 2005

Dear Agnes,

It was a delight to receive your letter. I figured it would not be easy for you to process all I've said so far. I don't imagine any of this will be easy for you. This is quite an extraordinary situation, and you are an exceptional person to have opened yourself to it. It is not hard for me, I must say. For the most part, with certain people, I am a very open individual—too open sometimes. There are places in me that I conceal but only for self-protection. Still you'll find my heart open to experience. And with you there is a certain obligation for me to be forthright because you, of all people, deserve that and so much more.

I agree with you when you say that anger only hurts the person who harbors it, but it still seems so hard to let go of when the wounds are still open. You've chosen not to hurt yourself and have managed to let it go. This comes with wisdom, perhaps, and strength—the strength to move beyond toxic emotions. I'm not sure that I possess that amount of wisdom or strength yet. I am still hurt and angry over so many things. So many. To those close to me, however, I choose to give love in all its purity and light. I try not to expose them to places in me that are still raw and immature. At one point in my life, those closest to me were the most prone to be hurt by me—until I learned how to love, until I learned that pain does not have to be a part of love, as I once believed it did.

There is no rush in when you write me back, Agnes. I am here. I won't be going anywhere anytime soon.

I'm glad Christopher's other grandmother is doing well. I don't expect her to be anything but hurt and angry. I think of you all very often, especially Pat's other children, your grandchildren. I'm glad to know that life has not defeated them. All the young kids I've known have ended up in prison like me, dead, or chained to dope and alcohol, so it is really good to hear that Pat's kids have survived. You must be extremely proud of your grandson and relieved that he made it back from Iraq in one piece.

I really wish Pat had listened to you when you cautioned her about letting me, an active addict at the time, come stay with her. I'm sure you've played those conversations through your mind often through the years. You know, I still can't really believe all of this. My intention had never been to hurt Pat or anyone else, for that matter. That must sound like crap coming from me, but it's true. I live with what I've done like some people live with a terminal disease. And now that my brother has died such an ugly death, I can understand more clearly how devastating this has been for you and your family.

Yes, the ripple effect. When the detective called my grandmother and told her what had happened, she literally had a heart attack. So many people have been hurt. My brother and my sister mourned me as if I were dead. I think that is what incarceration does, in a sense. A person goes to prison and it's like they've died. They're no longer around. They're gone.

Andre and my little sister, Erica, asked me why I left them at a time when they needed guidance and support. They needed a father, and I was the closest thing to it they had, despite my dysfunction. My sister has never seen me strung out or high, though. My brother saw me once during one of my darkest days. I was asleep in my truck, which I'd just wrecked, and he found me, woke me, fed me, and didn't say a thing about what was so obvious. He gave me love and compassion at a time when I was clinging to the end of my rope. What an example I was, right? I became our father, whom I hated because he'd chosen cocaine over us.

But that was the only time Andre saw me as an active addict. And that was by accident.

You're right, addiction is a prison too. I'm not sure about the concept of a person being free in prison. I understand why some would take the position of saying it's possible. It depends on the perspective, I guess. Some guys get into religion and wax poetic about being free in soul. But the reality is they aren't going to walk beyond those gates or walls unless they get on some kind of mental trip. At some point they've got to come back down to earth, and when they get back they're still in the same place—on lockdown.

I think I told you that I don't believe justice exists in this world, outside of a few exceptions. If there is an afterlife, it will be where justice is meted out. I've seen too much ugliness to believe in it. I've seen it thwarted too many times. I think that earth is the densest, most difficult realm for us to manifest in on our spiritual journey. It is fraught with strife and suffering. There is joy, of course, but it is always so fleeting. I know there are happy people here and there, but when you talk to them you realize they are totally oblivious to the world or downright delusional. Most people I have observed or known have struggled with life, struggled to take its lessons and move on to the next challenge. And the funny thing is, knowing joy only makes its departure more poignant and, at times, heartbreaking.

It's been so long since I've felt joy that I've forgotten what it's like. But I realize this is my karma. It is the fruit of the seeds I've sown, so, though I acknowledge it, I don't lament it. This, right now, is my fate, and I welcome it.

It is good that you speak out. You've saved more lives than you probably know by being open about your experiences and pain. You have much to teach. There is always someone who hears the voice crying out in the wilderness.

And, no—I didn't succeed in the death-by-cop thing, just the death-by-prison thing. But it comforts my family to know I'm alive. We can still communicate, you know. But, is that justice? That's what I've asked myself time and again. They can talk with me, but you can't talk with Pat and Chris, and I'm sure you've thought about that. If I were in your shoes, I'm sure I would. But perhaps I'd be able to find the strength to be compassionate. I'm not sure I could be as forgiving as you, however. This is truly extraordinary on your part.

Do you know one other thing that has been amazing to me? I remember one time I was watching some talk show, and they were talking to parents who abused their kids. I broke down—cried. Every time I got myself together, I'd wonder how some big, grown adult could hurt a small, defenseless child. I'd remember how my stepfather and mother would beat me with extension cords until I bled like a whipped slave, how they would punch and kick me and choke me; I'd remember how absolutely terrified I was as a child, completely terrified. And I'd think of some other kid going through that and I just cried and cried … And now, here I am—a child killer.

As I've said, I still can't believe any of this.

Yes, yes, yes—the Margaret Atwood piece, "Ancestors." I'm sorry that it troubled you. I sent it right after I got your first letter and before I knew who you were. When I learned you were Pat's mom and Chris's grandmother, I immediately regretted having sent it to you. The imagery is so dark; I knew you'd misinterpret my motive for sending it. That it made you think I was crazy is kind of funny to me now. But I was horrified at the time. I still think "Ancestors" is beautiful, though; and it is my favorite poem right now. Why? Because of what she is saying about love and the sacrifice it requires.

This image of the ancient Mayan priests offering a sacrifice to their gods so that they'd bless them with abundance and prosperity is dark. I realize this. But it's the idea Margaret explores of giving life for life that moves me.

> What they
> tried, we
> tried but could never do
> before, without blood, the killed
> heart, to take
> that risk, to offer life and remain
> alive, open yourself like this and become whole.

She presents the priest's sacrifice of life and blood as a metaphor for the risks two people take when they open to one another in love. They are doing what those ancient priests did: sacrifice. But in this post-postmodern age, there is no need for the blood, for the actual physical life. What is required is spiritual sacrifice. That sense of vulnerability, of openness, of communion with the gods, with spirit—this is what I see in this poem.

Yes, I admit it is disturbing. That's probably why I'm drawn to it. My tastes are not very conventional. I haven't read *The Handmaid's Tale*. I would probably like it. This poem is the only thing by Margaret Atwood I've ever gotten my hands on. It has made me a fan. It is so utterly pure, I think. I've read it countless times—hundreds, probably, and it never ceases to touch me. *Open yourself like this and become whole* takes me every time.

Because isn't that how you become whole? By opening yourself to love and trust and vulnerability?

I've enclosed something I wrote a couple of years ago. I haven't written about Pat or Chris. I doubt if I ever will. I think it would be disrespectful to them. Or perhaps, I am simply a coward and afraid. Perhaps.

Peace and blessings 2U,
Leonard

Now I Know

Now I know that I am a survivor.

Now I know that I survive.

Now I know that I have lived and am living a life like no other.

Now I know how very much I don't know, how much I have to learn.

Now I know that I will know what I need to know when life presents the challenge.

Now I know that crisis and opportunity can become one.

Now I know that I am on a journey of the moment.

Leonard

April 27, 2005

Dear Agnes,

I'm not as open with others as I am with you. As a writer, there is a certain amount of self-revelation that I indulge in, but there are limits. There are many things I won't write about or discuss.

I don't have very many friends for a multitude of reasons. But I am frank and forthright with those who are close to me. There is a saying that is used: "on my square." Your square is your life, your consciousness, your existence. It is what a person stands on and represents. If someone says a person is on his square, it means that person is inside his personal zone, his mental and spiritual space.

Well, I feel I owe those few people who are on my square honesty and disclosure. Open, direct communication can be both healing and enlightening. So I try to practice it with people on my square.

You, by nature of what connects us, are on my square. You are an integral part of my life, and vice versa. I don't feel you are out to attack me. I feel you are out for healing and learning. It's because of this that I've decided to approach our situation as I have.

No, I was not trying to get killed at Taylor CI in 2003. And I certainly wasn't trying to get executed. I'd learned to value my life by then—hadn't always done that. It was still a young, novel concept for me. Prior to a sort of spiritual epiphany I had in 2001, I'd lived on the verge of suicide every day of my life.

I'd been moments away from it that December's night in '01. I wanted to die. I was resolute, clear headed, and unemotional. I was simply done with being alive. I laughed on my bunk in the dark and told God I was a dead man at midnight if She didn't give me a sign that I was wrong.

I hadn't been paying attention to the conversation between a guard and a convict in the cell beside me, but something made me begin to listen. What I heard in the aftermath of my laughter at God cut a hole through the darkness and touched me.

"How do you know we don't choose to come to earth to learn? To use the pain to grow spiritually?" the guard asked the convict.

He spoke about Jesus without being cliché. I was reminded of the poem "Footprints." I'm sure you know the one. A woman dreams about walking along a beach with Jesus. When she looks at the footprints they made in the sand, she notices intervals where there were only one set of footprints. She's dismayed at first, assuming those lone footprints represent times that Jesus had abandoned her. When she questions him, he says, "Where you see only one set of footprints is where I carried you."

That got to me—punched a hole through my heart. If that wasn't a sign from God, Billie Holiday was the lamest chick to ever sing the blues.

I listened. I chose to live. It occurred to me that spirit had no intention of allowing me to leave earth with an unfulfilled mission.

By the way, our correspondence is clarifying that mission. Thank you.

But as for Charles and the Taylor CI situation in 2003, that was an incredible situation, Agnes. He attacked me. I protected myself. I had absolutely no intention of hurting the man as badly as he was hurt. I only wanted to survive. The unit sergeant had put me in a similar situation before, and I'd been able to handle it with finesse and intelligence. However, with Charles, things quickly spiraled beyond my control. When I was told he'd died (which was wrong, at the time), I just couldn't believe it. I did not want to be responsible for the loss of another life. I tore a piece of steel off the floor heater and cut my wrists. I wasn't trying to kill myself. But I had to do something and decided to do that.

As to whether Charles was physically threatening to me, any man on the attack in a locked cell is a threat. I am a very capable man in regard to self-defense, but I don't discount a man's ability to hurt me if he decides to try.

The incident with Charles instilled wariness in me to use violence to resolve conflict. When I was younger, I was the type of person to take a beating because I was afraid that fighting back would mean a more severe beating. (I learned that from my folks' beating me more severely if I resisted.) Also, I genuinely did not want to hurt anyone. I'd gotten into a fight with a kid when I was twelve or thirteen and broke his jaw. That scared me. I avoided fights religiously after that.

Violence is the only method of communication most of these men comprehend, however. They do not understand words. They only understand the power of the fist. It is unfortunate but true.

My experience with Charles has taught me the acute unpredictability of the consequences of violence. Since then I've resisted resolving conflict with violence, though there have been a couple of occasions when I thought it unavoidable. If I am attacked, I will defend myself, but I've developed a strong distaste for violence and severely limit my associations because of this. I realize that it takes far more strength and discipline to resolve conflict peacefully than it does to fight someone. I don't know how much I can swallow or how strong I can be in certain situations, but I am making a conscious effort to avert any conflict that could result in violence.

Contrary to the newspaper reports, I did not kill Charles. He was killed by careless guards who denied him health care for four hours despite the vehement protests of the duty nurse. He was killed by incompetent emergency medical technicians who screwed up a routine medical procedure, an intubation, which is nothing more complicated than the insertion of a tube down the throat.

Question: Let's say I've exaggerated the amount of time Charles was in the cell after our fight. For argument's sake, let's say he was only in there an hour before he got medical treatment. He died because a lack of oxygen to the brain caused him to go brain dead. He was alive when he left that cell. If the injuries I inflicted an hour previously had restricted his breathing so severely as to cause brain death, would he have been alive and conscious one hour after our fight? But the officials, knowing the truth, claimed that I killed Charles, and I was slammed for it.

I spent several months on Maximum Management, a virtual dungeon above Florida's death chamber on FSP's Q wing. Three men were executed in that chamber beneath my cell while I sat on my bunk thinking about how close I'd come to being one of them, strapped to a gurney and killed with a needle and chemical cocktail.

Though I'm still in solitary as result of the Charles incident, I haven't been nor will I be charged for Charles's death. None of those truly responsible for it have been made to answer for their crimes like the men who were killed beneath my cell were made to answer for theirs.

My lawsuit doesn't adequately address that need for justice. It does force the prison officials out of hiding, however. It forces them to own the fact that their own had everything to do with Charles's death.

Anyway, in regard to the victim/offender dialogue program you plan to implement, I will do whatever I can to support your efforts. In my experience, Florida's prison activist community is small and completely insular, but I'm sure some can be inspired through concerted effort. You have far more experience in this than I do, and I really would like to learn from you. I really would like to be an active participant in this. I feel it is something I am supposed to do, not for myself, but for others who are in emotional need.

Like you, of course, I can write, and I believe I can do it well enough to persuade people that healing is absolutely necessary for all those affected by crime and its consequences. I've spoken with you about my fledgling blog, which I'm calling Higher Ground.

There is a budding prison reform movement. It's an infant right now, Agnes, but it's growing. People are beginning to see that using prisons as warehouses does very little to curb the dysfunction in the lives of those incarcerated. The recidivism rate hovers at about 65 percent. That means that, of the 600,000 Americans who are released from prison this year, 390,000 of them will eventually victimize someone else or themselves and return to prison. The community is beginning to realize that the women and men they throw into prison cannot be held there forever and will confront society when they are released. Better for them to get help inside to minimize the chances of their returning to drug abuse or crime when released than to have their problems exacerbated by the cruel, unforgiving environment they suffer while locked up.

I think that this moment must be seized. We are all on the brink of enlightenment, and we must push to achieve it. I've decided to use what abilities I have to help push. My focus is on relationships and healing. Actually, it's what I know best. I think my relationships are testimony to the possibility for healing and forgiveness even in the harshest of circumstances.

I don't claim to be enlightened or even fully healed, but I do believe that I can help others achieve what I am working toward myself.

This is synchronicity, I think, because this program you envision fits right into where spirit has led me—reconciliation, responsibility, relationships, love. These are the focal points of the blog I've been thinking about for some time. And I'm beginning to believe it will be my life's work to foster them. I will write David Doerfler of Concentric Journeys and request his information.

Agnes, I am glad I've been able to give you a gift. I very literally owe you my life.

You've also given me a gift. You've reawakened me to life's possibilities to give, for no other reason than the joy of giving.

I'm not sure I fully understand everything that is going on right now—and I can't articulate it—but I am as present as you are and believe we are on the verge of something momentous.

Peace and Blessings, Agnes
Leonard

Epiphany

He refused to forgive himself.
He reconciled with life
while doing life.
The violence;
the brutality and years of questioning
that followed: Did he care?
Did she matter to him?

Then, in a moment,
reading his writing,
I knew he cared.
She mattered to him.

Seeking somehow
to make a difference,
to build bridges and open doors,
he became part of the solution.

Unbidden words, phrases,
and moments to ponder
these flickers of light dancing
in darkness.

May 11, 2005

Dear Agnes,

I agree that our correspondence is surreal—and overflowing with conflicted emotion.

Your favorite bridge is the Brooklyn Bridge? You've chosen quite a bridge. If I had to choose a favorite, it would be a rainbow. I know; it's silly and impractical, and a rainbow isn't *really* a bridge. But it does kind of connect two different points, and it can be quite brilliant and emotionally provocative. I mean, they've inspired all kinds of myths ... and when you see one stretched across the sky, you cannot help but be moved by it.

Silly, I know.

You speak of how human beings touch and are touched by all we encounter. I also believe in the interconnectedness of things. I'm excited about science's strides toward proving this. I recently heard an interview with a scientist on a show called *Coast to Coast*. He spoke of the discovery that two particles in two different places as far from one another as the equivalent of over ten million miles can be so related that one will be simultaneously affected by changes that the other experiences. If one is acted upon by an outside force, the other will immediately reflect its partner's reactions. The phenomenon is called quantum entanglement.

Entanglement lends credence to the idea that we are far more connected to everything in this universe than we are isolated from anything within it. We view ourselves as separate from everyone and everything around us, but that is a result of our brains' need to categorize and differentiate as it sorts through stimuli. We perceive what seems to divide us—the barriers of flesh, color, and space—because our senses are ill equipped to perceive how we are one. We are quantum. We are condensed fields of energy vibrating in a sea of energy. Any physicist worth her salt will tell you this.

Anyway, I believe you are right about everything you've said about forgiveness. The reason I reject any ideas about self-forgiveness is because I believe that such an act is profoundly selfish and makes a person feel somehow absolved of the wrong they've committed. Emotion cannot be absolution for wrong committed. If there is any absolution whatsoever, I believe it must be the result of a person's actions. That is the only way to atone, as far as I'm concerned.

I would never, ever, ever have dared to ask forgiveness from you, especially you, and especially Pat's children, Chris's father, or from anyone else who love them. I cringe at the thought. You are exceptional and have worked through some of your pain and grief in an extraordinary manner. But you are definitely the exception. And I consider the strength you've shown and the attitude you've adopted as an undeserved blessing to me—in the sense that our correspondence is a gift, not a burden, to me.

What did you mean when you said you knew I'd have an influence on others whether or not I accepted my responsibility?

I agree that many men inside need habilitation. It's the poverty, not only of the environment but of mind and spirit as well. Prisons are filled with poor people who continually make poor choices—poor, uneducated people. It almost amazes me how many men can't spell or form a complete sentence on paper. And if they can't write, it stands to reason that they're not likely to be able to read either. And if they can't read, then it means they are exposed to a limited number of ideas that will contradict what they see. They come from ghettos into prison without ever being exposed to something different. They've a limited idea of what's possible for them.

About the Bible verse, 1 Thessalonians 2:8, that your clergyman friend included in his letter to you: Aren't believers, as men or women, the Gospel themselves? Giving themselves, being of service, is far more apt an expression of Christ's teachings than preaching them. I've found that so many get caught up in the language, in the pontificating and self-righteousness that they forget that Christ's most profound expression of his ministry was his sacrificing himself for the edification of his students and all others who would find truth in what he taught.

I believe we, our own selves, are the Gospel. I'm the furthest thing from a preacher you can imagine, however, and have no authority to come to such conclusions besides having lived and loved and been human.

Oh—before I forget. There's something I've been thinking about: The questions you don't ask are as eloquent as the ones you do.

Anyway, I hope to hear from you again soon.

I'll close with a quote from a rock group called Tool: "This body holding me reminds me we are eternal: all this pain is an illusion."

I wish you peace and many blessings.
Leonard

On the Night of the Full Moon

On the night of the full moon, I returned to Tallahassee with Christopher, a sleepy child. We had driven long and far—he to a new place, me to a new responsibility.

As we got out of the car, he looked up. Wide awake now, eyes bright, he pointed to the sky. Just above the roof was a big, round, bright moon. It was a shimmering silver light in a navy sky. All around were tiny flickering stars, blinking while the moon smiled upon us. Two tired souls stared at the sky, each thinking our own thoughts—the small child and the woman bonding in the vast universe.

May 11, 2005

May 21, 2011

Agnes,

Hey. It was really wonderful getting your poems and letters in the mail. And I loved your collage. It and your poem "Wooden Bridge" gave me a deeper insight into your love for bridges. For you, a bridge is a point between two places that enables a person to rise above and observe the view below. It seems that, while you appreciate safety and pay close attention to it, there's part of you that, maybe not likes, but is comfortable with a proximity to danger. You haven't chosen life's safest roads to journey. In fact, this idea of a bridge being suspended in air by an arch of stone or wood or spirit or mind is a risky kind of concept. As a child I recall being terrified of going over certain kinds of bridges, afraid they'd fall beneath me and send me hurtling toward my death below. There's a certain risk a person takes when crossing any bridge. And an enormous amount of trust is involved in walking a bridge into the sky and over to another space.

I see all of this in your poem and in your collage. People, bridges, butterflies, doves, connections, journeys, metamorphosis, peace—it's all here.

However, I disagree with you on one point. I'm not sure that people will always treat you how you treat them. I do realize my present environment may not be the best place to make a judgment concerning the idea, but it's all I have to work with right now. And, I tell you, many of these men do not respect a man who will treat them with dignity and respect.

One thing I've noticed that amazes me is that prisoners will abuse, harass, and disrespect an officer who treats them like a human being but are humble before the officers who abuse and treat them like animals. It's amazing to me.

What I've learned is that it's dangerous to be nice or friendly with most of these men because they see it as weakness and try to exploit it. It's almost like they can't take someone treating them with dignity, kindness, and respect. Maybe they think that anyone who would treat them like that is a fool. Perhaps. I know that unconscious self-hate is epidemic here. I think prisoners instinctively hate anyone who acts as if they like them.

I haven't totally figured it out yet. But I do know that most of my peers respect nothing but aggression. They don't seem to understand that aggression has very little to do with strength or power. They don't see the strength in silence, humility, or kindness. These are alien concepts here.

In 1997, I taught an eleventh- and twelfth-grade social studies class of kids who'd been kicked out of school. These grown men remind me of those kids—no self-control, very short attention span, stunted cognitive powers. But these are my peers. I find myself disliking some of them at times, not because of who they are but because of what they do. Still I am connected to them. I'm in the same pickle they are in. For me, there's always the question of whether I'm being arrogant in separating myself from them. That's too much like my father: arrogant, unsympathetic, and self-centered. The thought that I could share some of those traits with him terrifies me.

So I try to stay humble. And it's hard. I don't always succeed.

This brings me back to your collage. I do treat others with justice and respect despite the fact that I don't often receive the same in return.

You've typed my letters? I have yours safe as well. And I will keep them safe. I consider this experience important. Important isn't the word. I don't know what the word for it is, and that's unusual. I'm rarely at a loss for the proper word to express a thought.

Chris was a sharp kid. I don't know, most times, if I should talk about him. I didn't know him well. But I remember him, of course—trusting, vulnerable, smart, and inquisitive. I've often asked myself, *How could you? Of all people, how could you?* And I've never had an answer.

Have you ever read or seen Shakespeare's *Othello*? Well, Othello's euphemism for murder was "put out the light." And nothing I've ever heard has been more apt an expression.

I remember Chris and know why he was loved so.

No, I don't remember our conversation in '96. What did you tell me?

Agnes, the night I left First Step, I got high. I was getting high the entire time I stayed with Pat. All of this is a blur. I was living on the edge of the Grand Canyon. I believed my relapse was well hidden. I don't remember what brought everything out, but I recall Pat being more of a friend to me than I deserved. I remember that nothing anyone could have said to me would have altered my choices, though. Only experience could do that. I've never been smart enough to take someone's word for a thing. I've got to see and find out for myself. I'd heard that crack is highly addictive. One time and you're hooked. My approach to it was, "Oh yeah? Bullshit. Give me that pipe and let me see."

Dumbest mistake of my life. None of the tragedy that followed would have happened if I hadn't given my life away to cocaine.

I'm glad you decided to write to me. I think it has been inevitable. I'd wanted to contact you, but the chaplain at Tomoka, the prison I was incarcerated in at the time, refused to send you a letter I'd proposed writing. I sat with him in his office and explained my position, saying I wanted to make contact. He humored me, belittled me in a vague sort of way, and ultimately refused me. So I gave it up.

But you made your choice and reached out to me, which took a lot of chutzpah, by the way, not knowing what you were going to get in return. I was floored when I read your second letter. Like, *Whoa. I don't believe this.* There was never a question about whether I'd write to you, not for a moment. But I was conscious of not wanting to hurt you any more than I already had. So I wanted to be careful, responsible, but clear and forthright.

The poem "Epiphany" is a painting. Like, this is how you see me in this moment. This is how you react to me, and the humanity in it is stunning. These incredible moments, terrible circumstances—there are such blues and shadows and specks of light here. I do see myself within your phrases, and I thank you for being gentle with me.

I don't write very many poems any more. In the past, that's all I wrote. And I thought I was an amazing poet until I started sending my stuff to 'zines. I experienced a lot of rejection. I managed to get some encouragement, but an editor at a magazine called *Epoch* said something that completely shattered my confidence. I've erased his statement from my mind, but the effect has been lasting. I have almost no desire at all to write poetry. That statement crushed that spirit in me.

So I turned my attention to essays and novels. I think I can communicate more effectively on those canvases. They are larger. I can be more coherent.

So, when I write about you, I will do it in an essay. I feel that ours is a momentous experience, one with the potential to help many, many people who are hurting. There is definitely art in it, because art is life, right? And the best art is life in its most exposed places or moments.

There is art in your life that you capture within your poems—wonderful poems; clear, clean poems. Do you read them to people? Are there poetry readings in your area? Or do you keep them hidden?

I pray your journey to David Doerfler's was a safe one. You should be there now as I write this. I'm sure your experience at the restorative justice retreat will be life altering and enlightening.

I really can't wait to hear from you afterward. In fact, this letter should be waiting in your PO box when you get home. So are you in your car reading this? Was the retreat wonderful for you? Was there a lot of light and warmth? Peace? A bit of pain too, I'd guess. But I hope the light cut through the darkness.

Well, I'll close now and wish you an abundant, provocative experience on your retreat.

Peace and Blessings 2U,
Leonard

Journey

On life's journey, I have met so many, many persons. Each is so different: ancestors, parents, aunts and uncles, contemporaries, sisters and brothers, spouses, lovers and friends, acquaintances, colleagues, and sojourners.

I've worked hard, fought battles, engaged in politics and brotherhood. I've known love, hate, violence, expectations and disappointments, fear and terror, and joy. I've heard music, read fact and fiction, made poetry. I've come to know God by many names.

I have descendants—children who watch over me from the universe, grandchildren around the world. I have young friends who join in my life.

In my life's journey, I've come to acknowledge dissonance and the occasional epiphany.

September 28, 2005

The Rebirth of Joy

You can't see the iron in her bones at first glance. Pass her on the street and you'd see a woman up in age, would perhaps write her off as living in the twilight of her years. You wouldn't see the keloided heart grown incurably sensitive by its scarring. You wouldn't see the children she's outlived—one claimed by AIDS, another by violence, another by SIDS. The addiction that bruised her was unable to defeat her. The war against cancer she fought and won was unable to diminish her. She has not been broken; she has refused to be ground to dust.

I met her for the first time outside of a Walmart in Sarasota, Florida. I was with her daughter, Pat, my lover at the time, and could only see the older woman who disapproved of the man too young and out of control for her little girl.

I cared little for her opinion.

We met again at Pat's apartment. She was not charmed by my ease in the kitchen. The pasta and chicken Alfredo I whipped up, the charm I used to disarm those most suspicious of my duplicity, were not enough to hide what was evident to her—that I was an active cocaine addict spiraling out of control and threatening to drag her daughter with me.

I still did not care for her opinion. And neither did Pat. It would cost us both.

The next time I would see Agnes would be in a courtroom. She'd look at me intermittently as she read a statement to the court that I barely listened to. She'd tell a judge she believed Pat's spirit had moved me to accept a plea agreement for life in prison rather than face a trial where I was likely to get the death penalty.

My attorney would whisper in my ear to distract me from what she was saying. "Don't look at her. Just stare straight ahead."

But I would see Agnes out of the corner of my eye—diminutive, slivers of silver in her hair, a tiny woman big enough to tell a judge to spare the life of the man who'd killed her daughter and grandson.

Eight years later and I'm still alive, doing life in prison. At times I've regretted not landing on death row. At least then we could get it over with. Life, I mean. Slip the needle in my vein, jam the poison into my bloodstream, and strip me of the guilt that still chokes the hell out of me, the useless remorse, the memories of smiles and laughter I'd once shared with Pat and Chris.

Lord knows I've wanted to kill myself sometimes, which is why I was so absolutely stunned when Agnes wrote me a letter. Wishing me peace. Saying nothing about the retribution I would have wanted were I in her place. I didn't know who she was at first. I'd never known her name. She was always "Pat's mom" to me. When I got her greeting card—it was small and cream colored, and on the front of it was a drawing of a dove holding a fig leaf—I was mystified. *Who the hell is Agnes Furey?* I thought.

If she were a woman seeking a pen pal, I wasn't interested. Too many head games. Besides, I was already in a committed relationship and happy. I didn't need any complications.

But she wasn't a pen pal. "I've been thinking of you for some time," she'd written. "I wish you peace."

This was obviously someone who knew me. And I was intrigued. Was she a lover I'd known and forgotten about? An old teacher? The friend of a friend? The mystery brought a dash of spice to my life of stone walls, steel doors, and monotony.

I wrote her.

Before I got a reply, I sent her a poem I'd fallen in love with—Margaret Atwood's "Book of Ancestors." Whoever this Agnes was, I wanted to share it with her simply because it is gorgeous, like the vibrant colors of a healing bruise.

The piece uses the images of human sacrifice and blood as the symbols of the price we pay for intimacy, for communion. It was apt. It spoke directly to our situation. But she wrote back, saying, "I can't believe you don't know who I am. I am Pat's mother, Chris's grandmother."

I was floored and instantly horrified about sending the poem. I knew she would misunderstand. It would seem like a sick, twisted taunting.

priests pressing his arms and hands
down, heart slashed from his opened

flesh, lifted to where
the sun, red and dilated
with his blood, glows in the still hungry sky

Later, she'd tell me she almost regretted writing me after receiving the poem. The blood and violence within it were glaring and deeply unsettling coming from me.

Sitting on my bunk, her short letter in my hand, my lips parted, heart yammering, I couldn't believe my stupidity. Then I couldn't believe the woman had chosen to write me.

I'd tried to contact her years earlier. I didn't know what I'd say, but there was a vague yet insistent impulse within me to make myself available to her.

The prison chaplain refused to make the connection, saying it was inappropriate. Perhaps he was right. What would I have said? No "I'm sorry" could change what I'd done or be balm for her grief.

In Margaret's poem, vulnerability and sacrifice are paths to communion. The priest cutting open the supplicant's chest, tearing out the heart, and offering it to the gods is heralded as the epitome of sacrifice.

The priest, in making his kill, is seeking relationship with the heavens. For him, blood—the symbol of life and vitality—must be shed to fertilize that relationship and to establish the priest's sincerity. It was proof of his devotion.

No offering given without pain is sacrifice, Margaret seems to be saying. Without hurt, the gesture is empty, a cop-out.

you are intact, you turn
towards me, your eyes, the eyes
intricate and easily bruised, you open
yourself to me gently, what they
tried, we
tried but could never do
before, without blood, the killed
heart, to take
that risk, to offer life and remain
alive, open yourself like this and become whole

Her poem moves from the image of the priest's bloody sacrifice to this vision of lovers in a room sharing space, devotion. A woman watches her lover, his throat and belly exposed to her dark fantasy. His physical vulnerability in a moment where trust flares bright stirs her, speaks to her of the deeper vulnerability of spirit required as sacrifice to the gods of their love.

Margaret understood that intimacy demands that we risk our lives, our sanity. If we are unable to tear our hearts from our chests and offer them as fertilizer for communion and relationship, we are not living. We are automatons making kind gestures to mask our inability to open, to make ourselves vulnerable, and to give the sacred room to breathe.

The only thing I was certain of when I wrote Agnes was that I would make Margaret's sacrifice. I wouldn't play it safe. I wouldn't speak with Agnes from behind the wall of a fortress. I would expose my throat and my belly and hand her the knife. My heart—this cluster of raw, meaty, and blood-filled emotions and thoughts swelling inside me—would be hers for the taking.

What else was there for me to do? I'd taken the last of her children and her youngest grandson. I could not give them back. I could not take her grief or their absence away. The only thing I had to give was myself and all that created me. Whether I be monster or fool, I belonged to her.

I was aware of the costs inherent in my opening to this experience but hoped that, as Margaret suggested, both Agnes and I would become whole by surrendering to it.

I'd be confronting the worst of me. While I was aware of the gravity of my crimes, I'd distanced myself from them. Pat and Chris lived with me; their eyes, their smiles, and the looks of disbelief when I attacked them were constant companions for me, always lurking behind some corner to accost me when I closed my eyes—always there, wreathed in the tendrils of cocaine smoke that obscured my past.

But I was never confronted with the anger and grief I'd created in those who loved Pat and Chris. It was easy for me to live without anyone around me knowing I'd killed a woman and a child. I didn't have to divulge my dirty secret to anyone. It was enough that I lived with Pat and Chris. I didn't have to compound my guilt by dealing with the judgments of people who knew what I'd done.

Writing Agnes would strip me of that anonymity. Here was the person hurt most deeply by my crimes, and I was to stand before her while she held a mirror to my face so that I could bear witness to my own ugliness. She'd say, *Look at me. See these bruises under my eyes, this scar over my chest where you punched through to wring the blood from my heart? See these broken bones that won't mend, the lines you've carved into my face? It's from you. You did this to me. You hurt me like this.*

That is what, in ordinary circumstances, may have happened.

But this is what actually happened.

"You are not a murderer," she said. "You are a man who has murdered. There is a difference."

With these words, written within the depths of our correspondence, Agnes banished a nagging lust for death that had haunted me for years. She hadn't written to shame me. Neither had she written to save me. Over time, I learned that she'd reached out to me to learn who I was so that she could make some sense of the tragedy that had devastated both of our lives.

It is so easy to demonize someone who has killed. The survivor sees the killer in court. She studies his face. *This is what a murderer looks like,* she thinks. *Ordinary. No horns jutting from his scalp. He just looks like … a man. What is ugly must live inside of him, coiled in his darkness like a venomous snake, waiting. Given the chance, it will spring, revealing its deadly purpose, ruining other lives.*

But not if I can help it. He will not kill again. He will not hurt someone else like he's hurt me.

Grief can be a hard, truculent experience. When aimed at its cause—the killer of a loved one—it often denies its target's humanity. To admit that this killer is a man or woman who has loved, who has been hurt, who has dreamed, and who has grieved would deprive the survivor of the anger that often masks grief.

Agnes didn't make that mistake. In the beginning, perhaps, she hurt more deeply for the wildness she allowed her grief. Without a focus for her anger that would have masked it, it had no place to go but inside her. Her contacting me was a part of the process of coming to terms with it and creating a space for more healing, more transformation.

Sharing our hurt and experiences did not automatically release Agnes from her grief or me from my shame. But it allowed us to grow in awareness and brought us into deeper contact with what we have felt and learned. Questions lingered for her that only I could answer. The enormity of my shame, from which I'd hidden behind a veil of silence, could only be eased by revealing it to her.

So we collided—like clouds. Through the spilling of our thoughts and emotions in the ink flowing over, perhaps, hundreds of letters, we merged. We did not hide. Much of what we said hurt. When she told me how she initially could not believe what the cops who'd brought the news of Pat and

Chris's deaths had said, I immediately understood how devastating that first moment was. The poem she wrote about it seared me. "Sometimes a moment is an eternity," she wrote. "No. You're talking about someone else. Not my daughter. Not my grandson. Go away."

I understood this space so clearly because of Andre's death. Enduring my own grief enabled me to empathize with Agnes's more deeply. When she talked about stuffing it, denying it for a time so she could continue to crawl out of bed each morning, I knew what she was speaking of.

For weeks after learning of Andre's death, I stuffed my face in my pillow and wept savagely. I was careful, however, to be quiet so that none of the other convicts could twist my grief into a weapon with which to shred me even more. On the tier, the me they could see was as hard and unaffected as ever. But when I was alone, I was Andre's big brother again, crying over the dreams we'd shared that had been burned to the ground, to ashes, like the remains of his body.

Agnes told me that she'd initially hidden her grief. She had locked it in a box and tucked it deep within so she could make it through each day without shattering. She'd lost nearly everyone in her family, had outlived them all. If she let the collected grief bubble to the surface, she wouldn't be capable of moving, she believed. She'd be motionless on her bed, the grief a gigantic slab of concrete crushing her chest, mashing the breath from her lungs, breaking her ribs.

She hid it to survive. And that almost killed her.

Shortly after Pat and Chris's deaths, Agnes became ill. She told me that her skin and eyes had turned the color of mustard.

When she visited a physician, she learned that her gallbladder had rotted and become dead chunks of useless flesh that needed to be removed. She'd stashed her locked box of grief into that organ, and it was nearly the death of her.

That near tragedy compelled her to unearth her pain. She could no longer afford to bury it. She had to allow it to be present. Part of this process included reaching for me and digging into these wounds, discovering what could be salvaged from these experiences, and running across bridges with this new knowledge into new worlds.

In Roman mythology, Hades becomes enraptured with a young maiden, Persephone, and kidnaps her as she's playing in a field of flowers. He imprisons her in his underworld, and her mother, Demeter, is ravaged by grief when she discovers the crime. As Mother Nature, she neglects the lilac, the spruce, and the hyacinth, and winter descends in her absence.

Zeus, bearing witness to Demeter's grief and the earth's emptiness, sends Hermes to free Persephone. Hermes does, but not before Hades feeds her an enchanted pomegranate, binding her to him for eternity. She's able to leave with Hermes to return to the earth's surface and rekindle Demeter's joy, but for six months of every year, because of Hades's treachery, Persephone must return to Hades and Demeter's resultant sorrow strips the earth of life, leaving it dead. Barren. Cold.

A hard, desolate, winter-beaten land is the consummate image to depict the emotional landscape of a person victimized by a criminal. The depression that ensues after being violated, having your sense of safety torn away, kills joy, or destroys summer. Demeter's grief, I think, is that of the survivor trying to hold it together in the aftermath of crime.

But when is it over? How do you get back what's been stolen from you? No one can survive an interminable winter. At some point, a person has got to begin yearning for the rejuvenating heat of the sun. One has got to begin to despise the cold, to hunger for restoration.

The woman who has been raped will rarely feel completely safe again. After time and a lot of work, perhaps, she may regain a sense of security. Maybe she stops expecting some guy to reach up from under her car and grab her ankle in the night. She may get over the alarm she feels, the fear she endures whenever a man touches her. But she can never go back to what life was for her before being raped. Her sense of security will always bear the scar of having been broken.

When Persephone returns to Demeter, she is not the same carefree girl she was before being kidnapped. She is still her mother's daughter, but she is forever altered by the time she's spent in hell. The poisoned fruit she was forced to eat while she was there will always be part of her story. It won't go away.

The land heals. Spring is born. But nothing is the same. The winter of the heart—depression—will at times return. Persephone is bound to the cycle of return inherent to having been victimized, as is Demeter. The anger, the fear, the shame, the terror, and the inarticulate hurt are nails pounded into the heart and left to rust.

Agnes and I reached into each other because the years had not removed the nails from our hearts. We'd worked alone to climb out of the hells we'd been in but were not completely free. Our liberation was incomplete because, without a Hermes to lift us over the chasm separating *knowing* from mystery, we were left with too many unanswered questions and too many unspoken words.

What Agnes and I discovered on our journey through the written word and cluttered corners of our hearts is that we, at varying times, could serve as the other's Hermes. Because, at its core, this has always been about restoration and reconciliation. That's why Persephone and Demeter's story is so relevant to ours. By making Margaret's sacrifice—by being open, receptive, vulnerable to each other, and unprejudiced about what our roles should be or what we'd find—we learned that both victim and survivor have some rescuing to do.

It isn't about the survivor's wearing the mask of the pious, unblemished *uber*-saint and being able to overlook his or her own pain to deliver the sinner from the muck and mire. It's about two individuals who are bound by tragedy seeking to understand it, this universe, and themselves by applying balm and bandages where their scabs are tender enough to break open and bleed.

Demeter's grief—the anger of loss—devastates the lives of both survivor and offender. This shared experience equips both, if they are capable of empathy and trust, to serve as the other's Hermes, to restore something of what has been lost. While nothing can ever be as it was, we can break winter. We can till the soil and bury seeds in warm, receptive earth. Life can bloom again. We can bathe in the heat and light of a new season knowing that while winter is sure to return, so will spring. So will joy.

April 2006

Becoming

Becoming. I am becoming, but what?
Becoming older, yet younger;
Becoming tired and more engaged;
Becoming a writer, becoming a poet;
Becoming again, perhaps, a woman;
Becoming quiet, becoming outraged;
Becoming outrageous;
Becoming a friend;
Becoming intimate;
Becoming honest;
Becoming afraid;
Becoming courageous;
Becoming silly;
Becoming healthy;
Becoming a cool grandma;
Becoming a mentor;
Becoming a student;
Becoming a listener;
Becoming a spectator;
Becoming a participant;
Becoming a healer;
Becoming healed.

September 14, 2005

So Much Depends Upon

So much depends upon geese resting on the water,
gray feathered wings floating softly.

So much depends upon wildflowers in the median—
Bright, tiny specks of red, pink, and yellow
beside the hot asphalt.

May 18, 2005

Epilogue

As I've learned from previous painful episodes in my life, wrenching pain must be faced and lived through, not ignored or stuffed or acted out in a rage. You get through it and use what you learn from your journey to help others. Women with breast cancer have made a difference in how that disease is treated. People living with HIV/AIDS have made many societal changes. Those of us who have survived violent crimes have a responsibility to do what we can to make a difference so as to minimize victimization where we can. Those who are in prison have a responsibility to put something positive back into the universe. They can make a difference for those who are in prison with them as well as with people in the larger community outside of prison. As I've witnessed Leonard's growth and experienced my own in our journey through these years, I've become more consciously aware of my responsibility to carry this message forward: *The only way through it is through it.*

This is the guiding principle of the organization Leonard and I have created, Achieve Higher Ground. The way through any difficulty, we believe, is to engage the challenge, find the meaning in it, use what you learn from it to grow and advance toward your higher ground, and then pay it forward. Our way of paying it forward has been to use our journey as inspiration for change.

So far we have succeeded in opening Florida's DOC to restorative justice practices. After meeting Hugh MacMillan, an activist and attorney who has been influential in the expansion of the character- and faith-based program model in Florida's DOC, I began to facilitate Circles of Restoration and Accountability (CORAs) within already existing programs at Wakulla Correctional Institution. We are expanding the CORA model, and Leonard is facilitating Florida's first restorative justice–centeric peer-to-peer program, Higher Ground, at Apalachee Correctional Institution, the prison he is now housed in.

This is the fruit of our relationship at work—transcendence, healing, redemption, justice. This is where the journey has taken us on our path to higher ground.

For more information, come see us at http://www.wildflowersinthemedian.com.

Afterword

WHY RESTORATIVE JUSTICE MATTERS

Restorative justice (RJ) invites those who have been victimized by crime to respond at the highest level of human evolution. Instead of adding hatred to an already violent action, those choosing RJ are actively seeking a path of peace. While it may seem incomprehensible for someone whose life has been devastated by the murder of their child—in this case, Agnes Furey—to want to meet the person who committed such a heinous crime, many parents want exactly that. Their grief, pain, and suffering transform them. They can no longer find the answers they seek in the traditional criminal justice system. Giving meaning to their child's life demands that they explore other avenues.

Our justice system asks what laws were broken and what punishment suits the crime. Legal negotiations often prevent the person who committed the crime from taking responsibility for his or her actions. While rehabilitation is the goal, recidivism rates indicate that incarceration rarely improves one's behavior or core value system. Overall, there is a disconnect created by our criminal justice system that impedes a criminal's accountability for his or her actions and precludes him or her from returning to society in a positive, sustainable manner. Finally, although some therapeutic programs exist, little support is offered to the victim, whose needs are overlooked.

Restorative justice, which is derived from traditions of indigenous peoples of New Zealand, Australia, and Canada, has at its core an abiding belief that a dignified response to crime will result in healing for all. While community protection is key, accountability and expressing remorse for one's actions by the person who committed the crime are central to the process. The victim's role is to determine an appropriate resolution, thus enabling him or her to move on with his or her life. It is in this realm that the parents of a murdered child may well ask to meet with the person who killed their child, and this can take place during incarceration.

Consider this paradigm shift: when a crime is committed, a relationship is established between individuals. While it is completely understandable why some want the "monster" who killed a family member to also die, violent action continues the cycle of violence. At our highest level of good, we are called upon to find the human-to-human connection. It is in this space, after taking a giant leap of faith, that transformation of heart, mind, and soul can occur.

Wildflowers in the Median represents the restorative journey of Agnes and Leonard. Theirs is a profoundly impactful tale of healing and redemption. While some may question the value of communication of this nature, the transformation each experiences through this connection is palpable in their correspondence.

Martha Weinstein is a social worker and certified mediator. She is the founder and former director of the Neighborhood Justice Center, a community mediation program with a restorative justice component.